GES

Ouvert en septembre 2007, ce premier 5 tridents réinvente un concept palace propre au Club. Esprit village, convivialité,

ZEN ATTITUDE

Shanti Ananda

DEMEURÉ LONGTEMPS SAUVAGE, VOUÉ À LA CANNE À SUCRE, LE SUD SE PARE DÉSORMAIS DE PALACES TRÈS ÉTOILÉS. OBLIGEANT, SUR LES AUTRES CÔTES, LES HÔTELS MYTHIQUES À REDORER LEUR BLASON. ZOOM SUR LES DERNIÈRES ADRESSES LES PLUS TRENDY DE L'ÎLE.

Cap au sud, une évidence. A Saint-Félix, Rivière des Galets. Escale au *Shanti Ananda*, copie balnéaire de son aîné himalayen. Avec pour ambition de s'affirmer comme la destination spa mauricienne. Aux grands rêves les grands moyens, 4 500 mètres carrés dédiés au corps et à l'esprit, entre forêt de palmes chuchotantes et vagues alanguies. Dès les premières lueurs du jour, les hôtes en apesanteur ondulent vers l'une des 17 cabines enchâssées dans un univers végétal et aquatique, pour goûter aux bienfaits ayurvédiques ou à la sensualité des massages. Au fil des jours, ponctués de pauses langoureuses dans les suites ou villas aux subtiles nuances sable, d'intermèdes gourmands autour d'une carte élaborée selon les principes holistiques, de confidences murmurées dans le salon de thé, les corps se délient et se métamorphosent. Sans l'ombre d'une privation, au contraire. Est-ce le secret du *Shanti Ananda* ? L'art de concilier prestations d'un palace, plaisirs nautiques d'un hôtel de mer, dépaysement tropical, enchantement d'une philosophie du bien-être. Puis, lorsque l'heure est au départ, d'inviter au retour prochain en ce sud mauricien encore embaumé du parfum caramélisé des cannes que l'on brûle (www.shantiananda.com).

■ **Partir :** *Directours, jusqu'au 15 avril, vols A-R, 9 j./7 n., petit déj. compris à partir de 2 247 € ; début juillet à partir de 1 957 € (www.directours.com).* ➤

La Plantation d'Albion

même le champagne, autorisant à mener la vie de château sans songer à la note finale. Implantée sur la côte ouest, préservée des pluies et des vents dominants, *La Plantation d'Albion* marie originalité d'un hébergement en chambres, suites ou villas très orientalistes, belle liste de sports, loisirs gratuits et table exceptionnelle. Certes, les buffets demeurent, mais doublés d'un service en chambre stylé. Certes l'ambiance est très cinq étoiles, mais non empesée. Et les familles sont, comme toujours, choyées. Un sans-faute tant dans le choix du site, grandiose, adossé à la montagne, en bordure d'une plage, que dans la décoration imaginée par Marc Hertrich, diplômé de l'école Boulle. Bois précieux, étoffes indiennes, marbre, équipement high-tech, salle de bains à ciel ouvert et jardin privé pour les suites, le nec plus ultra. Quant au spa, signé Cinq Mondes, organisé autour d'un patio planté de bambous, il multiplie les tentations. Ah ! les bains japonais d'arômes et de fleurs, presque un péché tellement c'est bon, et le hammam Mousson Tropicale, déstressant ! Loin du cliché du Club véhiculé par *Les Bronzés*.

■ **Partir :** *victime de son succès, par le bouche-à-oreille notamment, peu de dates disponibles – malgré ses 266 chambres – avant juin. Forfait à partir de 2 039,50 €, vols A-R, 9 j./7 n. pens. complète, open bar, snacking, sports, détente. www.clubmed.*

PHOTOS : ROBERTO BATTISTINI

BARCELONA

HOTELS & MORE

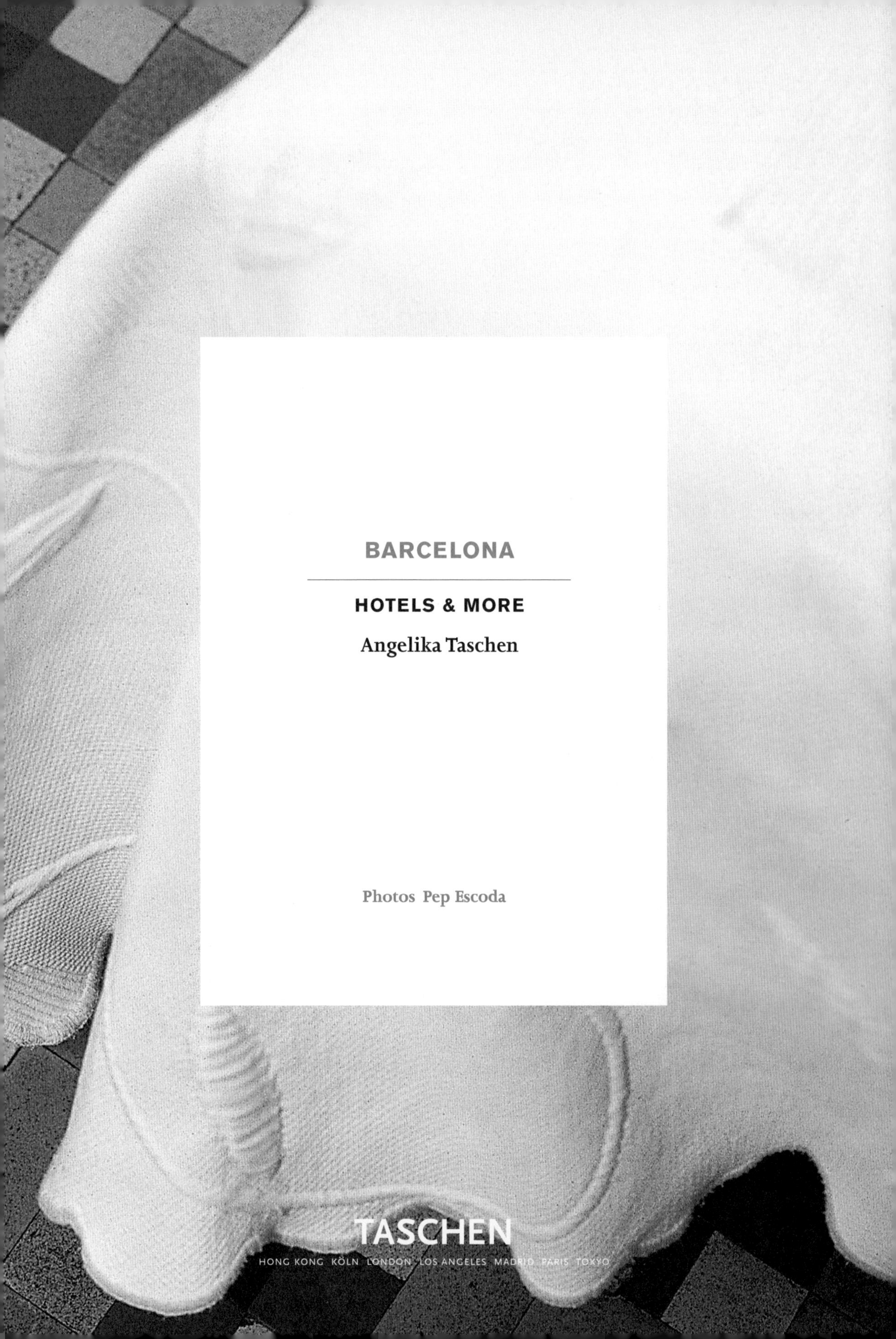

BARCELONA

HOTELS & MORE

Angelika Taschen

Photos Pep Escoda

TASCHEN

HONG KONG KÖLN LONDON LOS ANGELES MADRID PARIS TOKYO

This book is intended to encourage you to see more of Barcelona than just the main tourist attractions, like the Rambla, the Picasso Museum and the Gaudí buildings. I want to take you to the places where locals go, from authentic tapas bars like Quimet & Quimet and El Xampanyet, to atmospheric cafés tucked away in medieval courtyards with babbling fountains. And I want to introduce you to restaurants with world-class, creative cuisine à la Ferran Adrià. At least once in your life, you should experience the revolutionary culinary absurdity of lettuce with ice cream, risotto with condensed soil or a dessert that tastes like fresh tobacco.

Since the 1992 Olympics in Barcelona, many Catalans have been possessed – well, actually, more like obsessed – with a desire to be ultra-trendy and to design, design, design. Countless hotels, restaurants and stores have been stylishly revamped, some with great flair. But others, alas, have ended up looking characterless and bland. While researching this book, my goal was to select not only the best examples of classy, modern

Dieses Buch soll dazu dienen, dass Sie am Ende Ihres Barcelona-Besuchs nicht bloß die Rambla, das Picasso-Museum und die Bauwerke Gaudís gesehen haben. Es stellt Ihnen vielmehr authentische Tapas-Bars wie „Quimet & Quimet" und „El Xampanyet" vor, in denen Einheimische sitzen, Cafés in mittelalterlichen Innenhöfen mit plätschernden Brunnen, dazu Restaurants, die auf Weltniveau kreative Küche à la Ferran Adrià anbieten. Denn zumindest einmal sollten Sie die revolutionären Absurditäten probiert haben, wie z. B. Salat mit Eiscreme, Risotto mit kondensierter Erde oder ein Dessert, das nach frischem Tabak schmeckt.

Seit den Olympischen Spielen 1992 in Barcelona sind viele Katalanen von dem zuweilen etwas penetranten Wunsch beseelt, möglichst modern zu wirken und deshalb alles zu designen. Seither sind unzählige Hotels, Restaurants und Läden auf stylish getrimmt. Einiges ist gelungen, anderes leider mittelmäßig und seelenlos. Deshalb habe ich mich für dieses Buch auf die Suche gemacht nach dem Modernen mit

Ce livre est destiné à ceux qui ne veulent pas quitter Barcelone après n'avoir vu que La Rambla, le musée Picasso et les édifices de Gaudí. Il vous présente d'authentiques bars à tapas comme le « Quimet & Quimet » et le « Xampanyet » que fréquentent les autochtones, des cafés situés dans des cours intérieures médiévales où gazouillent des fontaines et des restaurants qui offrent une cuisine inventive de classe internationale, celle de Ferran Adrià par exemple. Une fois dans sa vie il faut goûter la salade à la crème glacée, le risotto à la terre condensée ou un dessert fleurant le tabac frais.

Depuis que les Jeux olympiques se sont déroulés à Barcelone en 1992, de nombreux Catalans, craignant de ne pas sembler assez modernes, ne pensent plus qu'au design. Depuis, d'innombrables hôtels, restaurants et boutiques ont dû subir leurs assauts stylistiques. Les résultats sont mitigés, certaines choses sont réussies, d'autres malheureusement médiocres et sans âme. En écrivant ce livre, j'ai donc souhaité recherché le moderne – mais avec de la classe –,

design, but also to steer you to those special places that have been charming their guests with ambience for decades, even centuries: old guest houses, cafés and restaurants that have largely retained their original character.

In spite of the current designer craze, visitors to Barcelona can still take a journey back in time. In the narrow little alleys of El Raval, Barri Gòtic or Sant Antoni you can stumble upon a shop that's hardly changed since it was built in 1761. On display inside are Catholic devotional items and very beautiful traditional christening and communion candles, which, back home, could grace a dinner table set in white. You might discover a store with a classic Spanish interior, where handmade espadrilles in every colour of the rainbow have been produced for more than a hundred years. The amazing smell of roasting coffee will lead you to Cafés El Magnífico, the coffee roaster who supplies Ferran Adrià with the world's finest beans. E & A Gispert probably has the only Roman-style roasting and

Niveau – und nach kaum veränderten alten Pensionen, Cafés und Restaurants, die den Gast mit Atmosphäre und Charme bezaubern.

Denn trotz des aktuellen Designfiebers erwartet die Besucher Barcelonas auch eine Zeitreise in die Vergangenheit. In den verwinkelten Gassen des El Raval, Barri Gòtic oder Sant Antoni findet der Besucher zum Beispiel einen original erhaltenen Laden aus dem Jahr 1761, in dem katholische Devotionalien und wunderschöne traditionelle Tauf- und Kommunionskerzen (die daheim einen weiß gedeckten Tisch höchst stilvoll schmücken) verkauft werden. Oder ein Geschäft mit klassisch spanischem Interieur, in dem seit mehr als hundert Jahren handgefertigte Espadrilles in allen Farben angeboten werden, sowie die einmalig riechende Kaffeerösterei „Cafés El Magnífico", die auch Ferran Adrià mit Weltklasseware beliefert. Bei E & A Gispert steht der einzige noch in Gebrauch befindliche Röst- und Dörrofen Europas. Dort kann man frisch getrocknetes Obst und Mandeln erstehen – mit

et les vieilles pensions, les cafés et les restaurants qui ont su garder leur charme et leur atmosphère d'antan et en font profiter leurs clients.

En effet, malgré cette fièvre du design qui s'est emparée de Barcelone, le visiteur va faire ici un voyage dans le temps. Dans les ruelles inextricables d'El Raval, du Barri Gòtic ou de Sant Antoni, il trouvera par exemple une échoppe datant de 1761 qui vend des objets de dévotion et de magnifiques cierges de baptême et de communion traditionnels (une décoration très élégante sur une table nappée de blanc), ou un magasin à l'intérieur classique offrant depuis plus d'un siècle des espadrilles de toutes les couleurs, ou encore la brûlerie de café odorante « Cafés El Magnífico » qui livre aussi à Ferran Adrià ses produits de qualité internationaux. C'est chez E & A Gispert que se trouve le dernier four de torréfaction et de séchage d'Europe. Vous n'oublierez pas de sitôt le goût des fruits secs et des amandes achetés ici.

drying oven still in use in Europe. Here you can buy freshly dried fruit and almonds with unforgettable flavour.

Expect some pleasant surprises when you check out the hotels in this book. The 1930s Spanish-style guest house Oliva, and the fin-de-siècle Girona, are just two examples of accommodation that's much less expensive and far more charming than many of the designer hotels that have proliferated in the last 20 years.

I can only hope that Barcelona preserves and cares for these historic treasures. What makes this city so special is its unique combination of ultra-modern and classic old-style design – not to mention the big-city atmosphere, sensational architecture, fantastic art and wonderful food enjoyed here on the coast under palm trees.

Adios amigos.

Aromen, an die Sie noch lange denken werden.

Auch bei der Übernachtungsfrage werden Sie mit diesem Buch Entdeckungen machen. Die Pension „Oliva" im Stil der spanischen 1930er und das „Girona" aus dem Fin de Siècle sind zum Beispiel sehr viel preiswerter und reizvoller als manche der Designhotels, die in den vergangenen zwanzig Jahren zu Dutzenden hochgezogen wurden.

Ich kann Barcelona nur wünschen, dass es diese alten Schätze hegt und pflegt, denn nur die einzigartige Mischung aus maximal modern und unverkorkst alt macht diese Stadt so besonders – mal abgesehen davon, dass man hier direkt am Meer unter Palmen Großstadtflair mit sensationeller Architektur, großartiger Kunst und köstlichstem Essen genießen kann.

Adios amigos.

Où passer la nuit? Vous ferez d'autres découvertes en lisant ce livre. La pension « Oliva », style années 1930, et l'hôtel « Girona », très fin de siècle, sont par exemple beaucoup moins onéreux et ont plus de charme que certains hôtels design qui ont poussé ici comme des champignons ces vingt dernières années.

Espérons que Barcelone saura veiller avec amour sur ces trésors, car c'est le mélange d'extrême modernité et d'ancienneté sans affectation qui rend cette ville si particulière – sans oublier, évidemment, le plaisir qu'offre, face à la mer sous les palmiers l'ambiance de la grande ville avec son architecture extraordinaire, ses chefs-d'œuvre artistiques et sa cuisine exquise.

Adios amigos.

El Raval

H1898

La Rambla, 109   08002 Barcelona
(entrance: Carrer del Pintor Fortuny)
☎ +34 93 552 95 52   📄 +34 93 552 95 50
1898@nnhotels.com   www.nnhotels.com
Metro: L1, L3 Catalunya
Booking: www.great-escapes-hotels.com

Designed in 1881 by the Catalan architect Josep Oriol Mestres, this building originally housed the Compañía General de Tabacos de Filipinas. Extensively refurbished and opened as H1898, this is one of the few new hotels in the city that hasn't been infected by the designer virus. The ambience harks back to colonial days. Photographer María Espeus went to the Philippines specifically to take photos of the local flora, and now her black and white motifs decorate the wallpaper and hang from the walls. All the rooms have polished wooden floors and a colour palette of green and white, red and white, grey and white, or simply black and white. The most attractive rooms have a terrace or balcony (my favourite is Junior Suite 628, which looks out to the Carrer del Pintor Fortuny). If that's a bit too pricey for you, then you can relax by the pool in a heavenly lounge chair on the roof terrace, and enjoy a stunning view.

Ursprünglich war dieses Gebäude der Hauptsitz der „Compañía General de Tabacos de Filipinas" – es wurde 1881 vom katalanischen Architekten Josep Oriol Mestres errichtet. Nach einer aufwendigen Renovierung eröffnete es als H1898 und als eines der wenigen neuen Hotels der Stadt, die nicht vom Designvirus infiziert wurden: Seine Atmosphäre wirkt vielmehr wie eine Hommage an koloniale Zeiten. Die Fotografin María Espeus reiste extra auf die Philippinen, um die tropische Flora aufzunehmen – ihre Schwarz-Weiß-Motive schmücken die Wände nun als Tapeten oder Bilder. Alle Zimmer haben Holzböden und sind in Grün-Weiß, Rot-Weiß, Grau- oder Schwarz-Weiß gehalten. Besonders schön finde ich die Räume mit Terrasse oder Balkon (mein Favorit ist die Junior Suite 628 mit Blick auf die Carrer del Pintor Fortuny). Wer sich das nicht leisten möchte, kann auf der Dachterrasse mit Pool entspannen: Die Aussicht ist umwerfend, und die Liegen sind wahre Himmelbetten.

Ancien siège de la Compañía General de Tabacos de Filipinas, ce bâtiment a été créé en 1881 par l'architecte catalan Josep Oriol Mestres. Rénové de fond en comble, il a ouvert ses portes sous le nom de « H1898 » et est l'un des rares nouveaux hôtels barcelonais à n'avoir pas contracté le virus du design – il rendrait plutôt hommage au style colonial. La photographe María Espeus s'est rendue spécialement aux Philippines pour y observer la flore tropicale – ses motifs en noir et blanc décorent les murs sous forme de photos ou de papier peint. Toutes les pièces ont des parquets et conjuguent le blanc et le vert, le rouge et le blanc, le gris ou le noir et le blanc. Les pièces dotées d'une terrasse ou d'un balcon me plaisent particulièrement (ma préférée est la Junior Suite 628 avec vue sur la Carrer del Pintor Fortuny). Mais on peut aussi se détendre sur le toit-terrasse où se trouve une piscine. La vue y est prodigieuse et les chaises-longues sont divinement confortables.

Rates: Single and double rooms from 250 €, junior suites from 500 €. Breakfast 19 €.
Rooms: 169 rooms and suites.
Cuisine: Mediterranean dishes are served in the minimalist-décor restaurant that has a view of La Rambla. The desserts are especially delicious.
History: Opened in 2005 in a beautifully refurbished 19th-century historical building that recalls Spain's colonial past.
X-Factor: The pool in the cellar vaults.
Internet: Free of charge (high-speed WLAN).

Preise: EZ/DZ ab 250, Junior Suite ab 500 €. Frühstück 19 €.
Zimmer: 169 Zimmer und Suiten.
Küche: Im minimalistisch designten Restaurant mit Blick auf die Rambla werden mediterrane Gerichte serviert; besonders gut sind die Desserts.
Geschichte: Die historische Fassade erzählt noch heute von der kolonialen Vergangenheit des Gebäudes.
X-Faktor: Der Pool im Gewölbekeller.
Internet: Kostenfrei (highspeed, WLAN).

Prix : Chambre simple/double à partir de 250 €, Junior Suite à partir de 500 €. Petit déjeuner 19 €.
Chambres : 169 chambres et suites.
Restauration : Cuisine méditerranéenne dans le restaurant au décor minimaliste avec vue sur La Rambla. Les desserts sont particulièrement savoureux.
Histoire : Ouvert en 2005. La façade historique raconte le passé colonial du bâtiment.
Le « petit plus » : La piscine dans la cave voûtée.
Internet : Gratuit (haut débit, WLAN).

1

2

3

1   Museum & architecture/Museum & Architektur/Musée & architecture

MACBA
Plaça dels Àngels 1
08001 Barcelona
Tel: + 34 93 412 08 10
www.macba.es
End of June to end of September:
Mon–Fri 11am–8pm (Tues until midnight, Sat from 10am), Sun 10am–3pm.
End of September to end of June:
Mon–Fri 11am–7pm, Sat 10am–8pm, Sun 10am–3pm. Closed on Tuesdays and holidays.
Metro: L1, L3 Catalunya; L2 Universitat

The spotless white Richard Meier-designed museum of contemporary art opened in 1995. The radiant building stands out like snow against the blue sky, revealing the influence of Le Corbusier in its gracious lines and curves. The heart of the building is the four-storey atrium with a zigzag ramp that leads up to the exhibition rooms. The museum has an excellent bookshop.

Das strahlend weiße Museum für zeitgenössische Kunst wurde von Richard Meier entworfen und 1995 eröffnet. Der helle Bau hebt sich wie Schnee vom blauen Himmel ab und zeigt mit seinem Wechselspiel aus geschwungenen und geraden Linien den Einfluss von Le Corbusier. Herzstück des Gebäudes ist das über alle vier Etagen gehende Atrium mit einer Zickzackrampe, über die man in die Ausstellungsräume gelangt. Zum Museum gehört eine ausgezeichnet sortierte Buchhandlung.

Dessiné par Richard Meier, le Musée d'art contemporain de Barcelone (MACBA) a été inauguré en 1995. D'une blancheur éclatante, il se découpe sur le bleu du ciel, et l'alternance de ses lignes courbes et droites montre l'influence de Le Corbusier. Mais le cœur du bâtiment est son atrium qui s'élève sur quatre étages et est doté d'une rampe en zigzag par laquelle on accède aux salles d'exposition. Une librairie au choix remarquable fait partie du musée.

2   Cocktail bar/Cocktailbar/Bar à cocktails

Boadas
Carrer dels Tallers 1
08002 Barcelona
Tel: +34 93 318 88 26
Mon–Sat midday–2am
Metro: L1, L3 Catalunya

This tiny, classic cocktail bar has remained unchanged since 1933, and is still family-owned. It's one of the last old establishments still thriving on the Rambla, at the junction with Carrer dels Tallers, an area that's been otherwise taken over by chains like Starbucks and McDonalds. The founder learned his trade in Havana's famous Hemingway haunt, La Floridita, where the daiquiri was created. Order one at the bar, and don't forget to take a look at the photos on the wall, which show the former owner with famous guests like Joan Miró.

Die winzige, klassische Cocktailbar ist seit 1933 unverändert und in Familienbesitz. Sie liegt wie ein Relikt der alten Zeit an der Rambla, Ecke Carrer dels Tallers – eine Gegend, in der inzwischen Ketten wie Starbucks und McDonalds Einzug gehalten haben. Der Gründer hat sein Handwerk in Hemingways Lieblingsbar gelernt, im La Floridita in Havanna. Bestellen Sie also am besten einen Daiquiri und betrachten Sie die Fotos an der Wand, die die ehemaligen Eigentümer und berühmte Besucher zeigen, unter ihnen Joan Miró.

Ce minuscule bar à cocktails classique n'a pas changé depuis 1933 et appartient toujours à la même famille. Situé sur La Rambla, au coin de la Carrer Tallers – un endroit où des chaînes comme Starbucks et McDonald's sont maintenant établies – il fait l'effet d'un vestige d'autrefois. Le fondateur a appris son métier dans le bar préféré d'Hemingway, La Floridita à La Havane. Commandez donc un Daiquiri et contemplez sur les murs les photographies des anciens propriétaires et des visiteurs célèbres, dont Joan Miró.

3   Herbalist/Kräuterladen/Herboristerie

Manantial de Salud
Carrer d'en Xuclà 23
08001 Barcelona
Tel: +34 93 301 14 44
www.manantial-salud.com
Mon–Fri 9am–2pm and 4pm–8pm, Sat 9am–2pm
Metro: L1, L3 Catalunya

Barcelona still has some old-world chemists and herbalist shops with original interiors intact. Some of these shops, like the mysterious Herboristeria del Rei, Carrer del Vidre, 1 Tenda (www.herboristeriadelrei.com), acquired royal protection a hundred or more years ago. You can find typical Catalan natural medicines in Manantial de Salud, too, ranging from essences claiming to cure impotence, to teas and cosmetics, to propolis and gelée royale. Stop by here, even if only to breath in the wonderful fragrance.

In Barcelona sind noch einige nostalgische Apotheken und Kräuterhandlungen mit antiken Interieurs erhalten. Es gibt Läden, die vor mehr als hundert oder zweihundert Jahren die königliche Protektion erlangten – wie die geheimnisvolle Herboristeria del Rei, Carrer del Vidre, 1 tenda (www.herboristeriadelrei.com). Auch bei Manantial de Salud kann man typisch katalanische Naturheilmittel finden: von Essenzen, die selbst Impotenz kurieren sollen, über Tees und Kosmetik bis zu Propolis und Gelée royale. Schon allein wegen des wunderbaren Duftes sollte man hier einmal hereinschauen.

À Barcelone, on trouve encore des pharmacies rétro et des herboristeries nichées dans des intérieurs anciens. Certaines boutiques sont placées sous la protection royale depuis plus d'un siècle ou deux. C'est le cas de la mystérieuse Herboristeria del Rei, Carrer del Vidre, 1 tenda (www.herboristeriadelrei.com). On peut trouver aussi des spécialités naturopathiques typiquement catalanes chez Manantial de Salud : essences contre l'impuissance, tisanes, soins cosmétiques, propolis et gelée royale. La boutique vaut

4

5

6

le détour rien qu'à cause des arômes merveilleux qu'elle exhale.

---

4 Cocktail bar/Cocktailbar/ Bar à cocktails

Bar Gimlet
Carrer del Rec 24
08001 Barcelona
Tel: +34 93 310 10 27
Mon–Sat 8pm–3am
Metro: L4 Jaume I

On week days, this classically beautiful cocktail bar is quiet – you may feel like you're in an Edward Hopper painting as you sit at the long mahogany bar. But the bar comes alive on Fridays and Saturdays, when Barcelona's trendsetters come to sample the professionally mixed cocktails and listen to jazz.

Unter der Woche ist es in dieser klassisch schönen Cocktailbar sehr ruhig – dann fühlt man sich am langen Mahagonitresen fast wie in einem Edward-Hopper-Gemälde. Am Freitag und Samstag wird die Bar richtig voll; Barcelonas Kulturszene schätzt die professionell gemixten Cocktails und die Jazzmusik.

Ce joli bar à cocktails classique est très tranquille en semaine – assis au long comptoir d'acajou, on se sent presque comme dans un tableau d'Edward Hopper. Mais le vendredi et le samedi, les clients affluent et on y est à l'étroit ; la scène culturelle de Barcelone apprécie les cocktails mixés avec art et le jazz.

---

5 Restaurant/Restaurant/Restaurant

Carmelitas
Carrer del Doctor Dou 1/
Carrer del Carme 42
08001 Barcelona
Tel: +34 93 412 46 84
www.carmelitas.biz
Daily 1.30pm–4pm and 9pm–midnight (Thurs–Sat to 1am)
Metro: L3 Liceu

This restaurant near the Boqueria market is in an old Carmelite convent, which explains the name. The airy modern and simple interiors were designed by Pilar Líbano. The food is similarly unfussy: the chef uses seasonal ingredients bought from the local market. The coffee is delicious, and Carmelitas sets the table with cloth napkins, an unusual, classy touch in an inexpensive restaurant. On warm days, guests can sit in Doctor Fleming's garden on the opposite side of the street.

Dieses Restaurant liegt in der Nähe des Boqueria-Marktes und ist in einem ehemaligen Karmeliterinnen-Konvent untergebracht – diesem Kloster verdankt es auch seinen Namen. Das Interieur im alten Gemäuer wurde von Pilar Líbano modern, luftig und ohne Firlefanz gestaltet. Ebenso unverschnörkelt ist das Essen: Der Küchenchef verwendet saisonale Zutaten aus der Region, die direkt vom Markt kommen. Der Kaffee schmeckt besonders köstlich, und man bekommt hier Stoffservietten, was in preiswerten Lokalen sonst nicht üblich ist. An warmen Tagen können die Gäste auch im gegenüberliegenden Garten des Doctor Fleming sitzen.

Sis dans un ancien couvent de carmélites, ce restaurant est situé à proximité du marché de la Boqueria. Grâce aux soins de Pilar Libano, l'intérieur est maintenant moderne, dégagé, sans fioritures. La cuisine est tout aussi sobre : le chef utilise des produits régionaux de la saison, achetés au marché. Le café est délicieux et on a ici des serviettes en tissu, ce qui n'est pas courant dans des établissements bon marché. Lorsqu'il fait chaud, les clients peuvent aussi s'asseoir en face, dans le jardin du Docteur Fleming.

---

6 Chocolate shop/Schokoladengeschäft/ Boutique de chocolats

Xocoa
Carrer de Petritxol 11-13
08002 Barcelona
Tel: +34 93 301 11 97
www.xocoa-bcn.com
Daily 9am–9pm
Metro: L3 Liceu

Although Xocoa was founded back in 1897, nowadays the company seems more avant-garde than traditional. Here you'll find the most unusual sweets in all of chocolate-mad Barcelona. Xocoa makes lavender, green tea, ginger, thyme and saffron chocolates, each variety packed in a distinctive retro-look wrapping. The chocolates are sold in minimalist boutiques as well on a new website. The brand is now so successful, it's expanded to13 shops in Spain, seven of which are in Barcelona. The branch at Carrer de Petritxol also has a café.

Xocoa wurde bereits 1897 gegründet; das Unternehmen zeigt sich heute aber eher avantgardistisch denn traditionell – hier gibt es die außergewöhnlichsten Süßigkeiten im schokoladeverrückten Barcelona: Schokolade mit Lavendel, grünem Tee, Ingwer, Thymian oder Safran, jede Sorte im schicken Retrolook unterschiedlich verpackt und in minimalistischen Boutiquen sowie auf einer jungen Website präsentiert. Die Marke ist heute so erfolgreich, dass es in Spanien bereits 13 Läden gibt, sieben davon in Barcelona. Hier in der Carrer de Petritxol finden Besucher außer der Boutique auch ein Café.

Fondée en 1897, cette « maison du chocolat » se montre aujourd'hui plus avant-gardiste que traditionnelle. On y trouve en effet les sucreries les plus insolites de Barcelone, ce qui n'est pas peu dire : chocolat à la lavande, au thé vert, au gingembre, au thym ou au safran, chaque sorte habillée d'un emballage rétro différent et présentée dans des boutiques minimalistes ainsi que sur un tout nouveau site Web. La marque a tant de succès qu'elle possède aujourd'hui treize boutiques en Espagne dont sept à Barcelone. Ici, à la Carrer de Petritxol, les visiteurs trouvent aussi un café à côté de la boutique.

Personal discoveries/Eigene Entdeckungen/Découvertes personnelles :

put cheese
e toaster
THANKS

BREAKFAST
Mon – Fri
7:30 – 10:00 am

Weekend
8:30 – 11:00 am

hostal gat xino

Hostal Gat Xino

Carrer de l'Hospital, 149–155   08001 Barcelona
☎ +34 93 324 88 33   📠 +34 93 324 88 34
hostalgatxino@gataccommodation.com
www.gataccommodation.com
Metro: L2 Sant Antoni; L3 Liceu
Booking: www.great-escapes-hotels.com

Hostal Gat Xino

The hotel chain Gat Accommodation opened its second hotel three years ago, and there are more European locations in the works (the next ones are planned for Madrid and Lisbon). The hotels in this chain are designed to fill a market gap for basic hotels with good service. The chain's corporate identity is signalled by a colour scheme of black, white and Granny Smith apple green, and by a cat's-eye logo ("gat" means cat in Catalan) that welcomes visitors to the hotel's website. The colour theme extends to the hotel's interior décor (it was designed by the young architectural office BOPBAA, which also designed the extension for the Thyssen-Bornemisza museum in Madrid). The designers have succeeded in creating a minimalist and functional interior that manages to be both modern and attractive. The hotel's service is also pretty minimalist, which is why the prices are low.

Das zweite Hotel der europaweit geplanten Kette Gat Accommodation wurde vor drei Jahren eröffnet (das erste Hostal befindet sich in Fußnähe und heißt Gat Raval, die nächsten Openings sind in Madrid sowie Lissabon geplant). Wie seine Schwesterhäuser möchte es die Marktlücke für eine einfache, aber gute Dienstleistung schließen. Für die entsprechende Corporate Identity sorgen die Farben Schwarz, Weiß und Granny-Smith-Apfelgrün – sowohl auf der Website, die Besucher mit einem grünen Katzenauge begrüßt („gat" bedeutet Katze auf katalanisch; es ist zugleich das Logo des Unternehmens), als auch bei der Inneneinrichtung. Diese wurde von dem jungen Architekturbüro BOPBAA übernommen, das unter anderem den Erweiterungsbau der Thyssen-Bornemisza-Sammlung in Madrid entwarf. Die Designer haben die Idee, das Interieur minimal und funktional, aber zugleich modern und schön zu gestalten, erfolgreich umgesetzt. Der Service ist ebenfalls minimal, so bleiben die Preise niedrig.

Le second hôtel de la chaîne « Gat Accommodation » qui veut s'implanter dans toute l'Europe a été ouvert il y a trois ans (le premier, « Gat Raval » est à quelques pas, les prochaines ouvertures sont prévues à Madrid et Lisbonne). Comme ses maisons-sœurs, il veut remplir un créneau en proposant des services simples mais de qualité. Pour ce qui est de l'image de marque, les couleurs noir, blanc et vert pomme granny smith y veillent – aussi bien sur le site Web qui salue les visiteurs avec un œil de chat (« gat » signifie chat en catalan; c'est aussi le logo de l'entreprise) que dans la décoration intérieure. Celle-ci a été réalisée par le jeune bureau d'architectes BOPBAA qui a conçu entre autres l'extension de la Collection Thyssen-Bornemisza à Madrid. Les designers ont réussi à traduire leur idée d'un intérieur minimal et fonctionnel qui soit aussi moderne et beau. Le service est lui aussi minimal, ce qui fait du bien au porte-monnaie.

Rates: Single rooms from 66 €, double rooms from 84 €, suites from 110 €, including breakfast.
Rooms: 34 rooms, 1 suite.
Cuisine: Mediterranean breakfast served on the small, wood-panelled patio, weather permitting. No in-house restaurant for lunch or dinner.
History: Opened in July 2004.
X-Factor: The website has great tips for restaurants, bars, clubs and boutiques.
Internet: 15 minutes for 80 cents (high-speed, WLAN).

Preise: EZ ab 66 €, DZ ab 84 €, Suite ab 110 €, inklusive Frühstück.
Zimmer: 34 Zimmer, 1 Suite.
Küche: Im kleinen, mit Holz verkleideten Patio wird ein mediterranes Frühstück serviert (wenn es nicht zu kalt ist). Ein Restaurant für Lunch und Dinner gibt es nicht.
Geschichte: Im Juli 2004 eröffnet.
X-Faktor: Die Tipps für Restaurants, Bars, Clubs und Boutiquen auf der Website.
Internet: 15 Minuten für 80 Cent (high-speed, WLAN).

Prix : Chambre simple à partir de 66 €, double à partir de 84 €, suite à partir de 110 €, petit déjeuner inclus.
Chambres : 34 chambres, 1 suite.
Restauration : Un petit déjeuner méditerranéen est servi dans le petit patio lambrissé (s'il ne fait pas froid). Pas de restaurant pour le déjeuner et le dîner.
Histoire : Ouvert en juillet 2004.
Le « petit plus » : Le site Web donne des tuyaux sur les restaurants, les bars, les clubs et les boutiques.
Internet : 15 minutes 80 centimes (haut débit, WLAN).

1   2   3

---

1   Club with restaurant & bar/
Club mit Restaurant & Bar/
Club avec restaurant & bar

Club 13
Plaça Reial 13
08002 Barcelona
Tel: +34 93 317 23 52
www.club13bcn.com
Restaurant open daily 8pm–midnight
Metro: L3 Liceu/Drassanes

Beautiful Plaça Reial, with its harmonious proportions, palm trees, Fountain of the Three Graces and street lamps designed by Gaudí, is almost inaccessible in the daytime because of the crowds – but at night it certainly comes into its own! It is a good idea to go to Club 13 after 11pm. The restaurant, bar and club all have splendid views of the Plaça Reial. The club, which occupies the former premises of a Capuchin convent, has four differently designed "Salas", where internationally renowned DJs play house music in the red-gold rooms. If you are too tired to dance, just relax with a cocktail on one of the comfortable sofas in the chill-out room.

Tagsüber ist die wunderschöne Plaça Reial mit ihren harmonischen Proportionen, den Palmen, dem Brunnen der drei Grazien und den von Gaudí entworfenen Straßenlaternen vor lauter Menschen leider kaum zu sehen – dafür aber nachts! Am besten geht man nach 23 Uhr in den Club 13, der über vier unterschiedlich gestaltete „salas" verfügt. Das Gebäude war früher ein Konvent der Kapuziner und bietet heute sowohl vom Restaurant als auch von der Bar und vom Club aus herrliche Blicke auf die Plaça Reial. In den rot-goldenen Interieurs legen renommierte internationale DJs House Music auf. Wer zu müde zum Tanzen ist, kann im Chill-out-Raum auf weichen Sofas bei einem Cocktail entspannen.

Pendant la journée, il y a tellement de monde sur la Plaça Reial que l'on distingue à peine ses proportions harmonieuses, ses palmiers, sa fontaine aux trois Grâces et ses lampadaires signés Gaudí. Mais la nuit sa splendeur saute aux yeux. Pour bien faire, il faut arriver après 23 h au « Club 13 » qui possède quatre « salas » différentes. Le bâtiment abritait autrefois un couvent de capucins et la vue sur la Plaça Reial y est magnifique, aussi bien du restaurant que du bar et du club. Dans les salles rouges et or, de grands DJs internationaux nous font écouter de la House Music. Celui qui est trop fatigué pour danser peut se détendre dans le chill-out sur des canapés moelleux en buvant un cocktail.

---

2   Vintage furniture/Vintage-Möbel/
Mobilier vintage

Gotham
Carrer de Cervantes 7
08002 Barcelona
Tel: +34 93 412 46 47
www.gotham-bcn.com
Daily 10.30am–2pm and 5pm–8.30pm
Metro: L3 Liceu; L4 Jaume I

Gotham specialises in vintage furniture and new editions of classic pieces from the '30s, '50s, '60s and '70s, with a special emphasis on the '50s. The atmosphere is very laid-back, as they also sell "dubious" reproductions. Commercial and TV art directors rent props from here, and this is where Pedro Almodóvar found many of the campy pieces for his film *Todo sobre mi madre* (All about My Mother).

Gotham ist auf Vintage-Möbel und Re-Editionen von Klassikern der 1930er, 1950er, 1960er und 1970er spezialisiert – mit Betonung auf die Fifties. Da man hier auch „unseriöse" Reproduktionen verkauft, ist die Atmosphäre sehr entspannt. Stylisten für Werbe- und TV-Produktionen, aber auch Star-Regisseure leihen sich in diesem Laden Requisiten für ihre Filme; Pedro Almodóvar zum Beispiel wurde hier für „Alles über meine Mutter" (Todo sobre mi madre) fündig.

Gotham est un spécialiste des meubles vintage et de la réédition de classiques des années 1930, 1950, 1960 et 1970 – l'accent étant mis sur les fifties. On y vend aussi des reproductions pas sérieuses et l'ambiance est très détendue. Les stylistes travaillant sur des productions publicitaires ou destinées à la télévision, mais aussi des réalisateurs stars viennent y louer des accessoires ; ainsi Pedro Almodóvar est venu faire un tour ici avant de tourner « Tout sur ma mère ».

---

3   Spanish fashion/Spanische Mode/
Mode espagnole

Como Agua de Mayo
Carrer de l'Argenteria 43
08003 Barcelona
Tel: +34 93 310 64 41
Mon–Sat 10am–8.30pm
Metro: L4 Jaume I

This charming little designer boutique sells accessories, shoes and clothes by Spain's most important style gurus, including Josep Font, Ailanto, Miriam Ocariz, Elisa Aman and Lydia Delgado. Here's where you'll find shoes by designers like Dorotea, Otto et Moi and Blay. A visit here is the best way to get an overview of contemporary Spanish fashion in a single stop.

Diese kleine, charmante Designerboutique führt Accessoires, Schuhe und Kleidung aller wichtigen Modemacher Spaniens – darunter Josep Font, Ailanto, Miriam Ocariz, Elisa Aman und Lydia Delgado – sowie Schuhe von Dorotea, Otto et Moi, Blay u. a. So kann man sich in einem einzigen Laden einen guten Überblick über die zeitgenössische spanische Mode verschaffen.

Cette charmante petite boutique design vend des accessoires, des chaussures et des vêtements qu'ont signés tous les grands de la mode en Espagne – par exemple Josep Font, Ailanto, Miriam Ocariz, Elisa Aman et Lydia Delgado – ainsi que Dorotea, Otto et Moi, Blay, entre autres, pour les chaussures. On peut ainsi se faire une idée de la mode espagnole contemporaine dans un seul magasin.

---

4   Delicatessen/Delikatessen/Épicerie

Can Ravell
Carrer d'Aragó 313
08009 Barcelona
Tel: +34 93 457 51 14
www.ravell.com

4

5

Sat/Mon 10am–6pm, Tues/Wed 10am–9pm, Thurs/Fri 10am–10pm
Metro: L4 Girona

Founded by Ignasi Ravell in 1929, the same year the World's Fair was held in Barcelona, this is yet another one of the city's long-running family businesses. Here you'll find top-quality goods from diverse regions: ham, anchovies, olives, cheese, tinned food, numerous oils, vinegar, wine, fine whiskies and liqueurs. Take your culinary delicacies upstairs and enjoy them while rubbing shoulders with the city's gourmets, artists, writers and intellectuals.

Ein weiteres der vielen Etablissements in Barcelona, das seit seiner Gründung in Familienbesitz ist – es wurde im Weltaus-stellungsjahr 1929 von Ignasi Ravell eröffnet. Nur Waren allererster Qualität aus den unterschiedlichsten Regionen werden hier verkauft: Schinken, Anchovis, Oliven, Käse, Konserven, Öle, Essig, Weine, Whiskeys und Liköre der Spitzenklasse. Im oberen Stockwerk kann man all diese Köstlichkeiten exquisit zubereitet genießen – Gourmets, Künstler, Schriftsteller und Intellektuelle sitzen hier Ellbogen an Ellbogen.

Encore un des nombreux établissements de Barcelone resté dans la famille depuis sa fondation par Ignasi Ravell en 1929 – l'année de l'Exposition universelle. On ne vend ici que des produits haut de gamme en provenance des régions les plus diver-ses : jambon, anchois, olives, fromages, conserves, huiles, vinaigres, vins, whisky et liqueurs. On peut savourer ces délices à l'étage supérieur. Ce que font les gourmets, les artistes, les écrivains et les intellectuels assis coude à coude.

5   Sexy espadrilles/Sexy Espadrilles/
     Espadrilles sexy

Cristina Castañer
Carrer del Mestre Nicolau 23
08021 Barcelona
Tel: +34 93 414 24 28
www.castaner.com
Mon–Sat 10.30am–8.15pm
Metro: L6 Muntaner

This business has been in existence for as long as the Castañer family has been around. But it wasn't until the '60s, when Yves Saint Laurent commissioned a pair of high-heeled espadrilles, that the Castañer business became what it is today. They no longer produce old-fashioned, folksy slip-ons, but luxury shoes with sex appeal and star quality. I would never wear any "espardenyes" but the ones made by Cristina Castañer.

Dieses Unternehmen existiert, seit die Familie Castañer existiert. Aber erst in den 1960ern, als Yves Saint Laurent ein Paar Espadrilles mit hohem Absatz bei Castañer in Auftrag gab, wurde die Firma zu dem, was sie heute ist. Hier produziert man keine volkstümlich-altmodischen Schlappen mehr, sondern Luxusschuhe mit Sexappeal und Starqualitäten. Wenn ich „espardenyes" trage, dann nur die von Cristina Castañer.

Cette entreprise existe depuis qu'existe la famille Castañer. Mais la maison n'est devenue ce qu'elle est qu'au cours des années 1960 quand Yves Saint Laurent lui commanda une paire d'espadrilles à semelles compensées. Pas de vieilles espadrilles folklo ici mais des chaussures de luxe, des chaussures de star avec du sex-appeal. Il m'arrive de porter des « espardenyes », mais alors uniquement celles de Cristina Castañer.

Personal discoveries/Eigene Entdeckungen/Découvertes personnelles :

El Raval

1   Architecture & art books/Architektur- & Kunstbücher/
Livres d'architecture et d'art
Ras

2   Restaurant & café/Restaurant & Café/Restaurant & café
Mamacafé

3   Cooks' apparel/Gastronomiebekleidung/Vêtements de cuisine
Sastrería El Transwaal

4   Market hall/Markthalle/Halle de marché
Mercat de la Boqueria

5   Suizos & churros/Suizos & Churros/Suizos & churros
Granja La Pallaresa

1   Oasis/Oase/Oasis
Jardins de la Universitat

2   Cocoa & milk bar/Kakao- & Milchbar/Bar à lait & cacao
Granja M. Viader

3   Haberdashery & interior/Kurzwaren & Interieur/
Mercerie & intérieur
Curtidos Pinós

4   Bakery/Bäckerei/Boulangerie
Barcelona Reykjavík

5   Garden café/Gartencafé/Café-jardin
El Jardí

6   Sports club & swimming pool/Sportclub & Schwimmbad/
Club sportif & Piscine
Club Natació Atlètic-Barceloneta

1   Catalan architecture & interior/Katalanische Architektur &
Interieur/Architecture catalane & intérieur
Hotel España

2   Market bar/Marktbar/Bar du marché
Bar Pinotxo

3   Coffee roasters/Kaffeerösterei/Torréfaction
La Portorriqueña

4   Pastry shop/Konditorei/Pâtisserie
Escribà

5   Café & bar/Café & Bar/Café & bar
Bar Lobo

Casa Camper

Carrer d'Elisabets, 11   08001 Barcelona
☎ +34 93 342 62 80   ☐ +34 93 342 75 63
barcelona@casacamper.com
www.casacamper.com
Metro: L1, L3 Catalunya
Booking: www.great-escapes-hotels.com

Casa Camper

Camper shoes are Spain's light-hearted answer to Germany's sombre Birkenstocks. The company was founded on Mallorca 120 years ago. But the original Camper shoe was designed by Lorenzo Fluxà in 1975 – the shoe symbolises an ecologically aware lifestyle that combines freedom, comfort and creativity. The first Camper shoe store opened in 1981, and in 2005 the concept was expanded and translated into a unique hotel. The 25-room Casa Camper was designed by Fernando Amat (Vinçon) and Jordi Tió. Each room has its own extra room: a quiet sleeping area that faces the back, and looks out to an 18-metre-tall vertical garden with 117 aspidistras. The sitting room, which boasts a hammock, faces the front. Bicycles, which can be hired for excursions, hang from the lobby ceiling. The Casa Camper offers a 24-hour snack service free of charge – but don't forget there are lots of good restaurants nearby!

Schuhe von Camper sind die spanische, humorvolle Antwort auf die strengen deutschen Birkenstock-Schuhe. Das Unternehmen wurde vor 120 Jahren auf Mallorca gegründet, den eigentlichen Camper-Schuh entwarf Lorenzo Fluxà erst 1975 – als Symbol eines ökofreundlichen Lifestyle, der Freiheit, Komfort und Kreativität widerspiegeln sollte. 1981 eröffnete der erste Camper-Schuhladen in Barcelona, 2005 kam ein Hotel mit einzigartigem Konzept dazu: Die Casa Camper wurde von Fernando Amat (Vinçon) und Jordi Tió gestaltet und hat 25 Zimmer. Jedes Zimmer besteht aus zwei Räumen – nach hinten geht ein ruhiger Schlafbereich mit Blick auf den 18 Meter hohen vertikalen Garten aus 117 Schusterpalmen, nach vorne eine Lounge mit Hängematte. In der Lobby hängen Fahrräder von der Decke, die für Ausflüge verliehen werden. Die Casa Camper bietet einen kostenlosen 24-Stunden-Imbiss; doch deswegen sollte man sich die vielen guten Restaurants in der Nähe nicht entgehen lassen.

Les chaussures Camper sont la réponse espagnole aux Birkenstock allemandes, en plus drôle. L'entreprise a vu le jour à Majorque il y a cent-vingt ans, mais la chaussure Camper – symbole d'un style de vie respectueux de l'environnement, d'anticonformisme, de confort et de créativité – n'a été créée par Lorenzo Fluxà qu'en 1975. Le premier magasin de chaussures Camper a ouvert ses portes à Barcelone en 1981, puis la Casa Camper a vu le jour en 2005 : un hôtel au concept unique en son genre, aménagé par Fernando Amat (Vinçon) et Jordi Tió. Il dispose de vingt-cinq chambres composées de deux pièces – à l'arrière une zone de sommeil avec vue sur le jardin vertical de dix-huit mètres de haut composé de cent-dix-sept aspidistras, à l'avant un salon avec hamac. À la réception, on peut louer les bicyclettes accrochées au plafond. Un buffet gratuit est ouvert à toute heure du jour et de la nuit – mais les bons restaurants abondent à proximité.

Rates: Single rooms from 202 €, double rooms from 225 €, suites from 245 € with double occupancy, including breakfast.
Rooms: 25 rooms and suites.
Cuisine: Free 24-hour snack buffet (sandwiches, salads etc.).
History: A 19th-century building transformed into an unconventional designer hotel with an environmentally friendly philosophy.
X-Factor: The Casa Camper is a non-smoking hotel.
Internet: Free of charge (high-speed, WLAN).

Preise: EZ ab 202 €, DZ ab 220 €, Suite als EZ ab 225 €, Suite als DZ ab 245 €; inklusive Frühstück.
Zimmer: 25 Zimmer und Suiten.
Küche: Das kostenfreie Snack-Büfett ist rund um die Uhr geöffnet. Es bietet u. a. Sandwiches und Salate.
Geschichte: In einem Haus aus dem 19. Jahrhundert entstand ein unkonventionelles Designhotel mit umweltfreundlicher Philosophie.
X-Faktor: Die Casa Camper ist Nichtraucherzone.
Internet: Kostenfrei (highspeed, WLAN).

Prix : Chambre simple à partir de 202 €, double à partir de 220 €, suite simple à partir de 225 €, double à partir de 245 € ; petit déjeuner inclus.
Chambres : 25 chambres et suites.
Restauration : Buffet self-service gratuit, ouvert 24 h sur 24 h. Il offre entre autres des sandwichs et des salades.
Histoire : Un hôtel design non conventionnel à la philosophie écologique a vu le jour dans une maison XIXe.
Le « petit plus » : Établissement non-fumeur.
Internet : Gratuit (haut débit, WLAN).

1

2

3

1   Architecture & art books/
    Architektur- & Kunstbücher/
    Livres d'architecture et d'art

Ras
Carrer del Doctor Dou 10
08001 Barcelona
Tel: +34 93 412 71 99
www.rasbcn.com
Tues–Fri 11am–9pm
Metro: L3 Liceu; L1, L2 Catalunya

The modern polycarbonate shelves in this
bookshop are filled with avant-garde books
about art, photography and design. In addition, Ras offers a select range of books
and journals on avant-garde fashion and
design. All of this is under the auspices of
the Studio Actar, renowned in Barcelona
for its ultra-modern book designs.

Die modernen Polycarbonatregale in diesem
Buchladen sind mit avantgardistischen
Titeln über Kunst, Fotografie und Design
gefüllt, zudem bietet Ras ein ausgewähltes
Sortiment und Zeitschriften über Avant-
garde-Mode und Design. Das Ganze steht
unter der Ägide des Studio Actar, das in
Barcelona für seine ultramodernen Buch-
entwürfe bekannt ist.

Les étagères modernes en polycarbonate
sont remplies de livres avant-gardistes sur
l'art, la photographie et le design. Ras offre
en outre une sélection de magazines
consacrés à la mode d'avant-garde et au
design. L'ensemble est sous l'égide du
Studio Actar, connu à Barcelone pour ses
designs livresques ultramodernes.

2   Restaurant & café/Restaurant & Café/
    Restaurant & café

Mamacafé
Carrer del Doctor Dou 10
08001 Barcelona
Tel: +34 93 301 29 40
www.mamacaferestaurant.com
Mon–Sat 1pm–midnight (Sun from 8pm)
Metro: L3 Liceu

There's no shortage of restaurants in hip
Raval, but few can be recommended as

highly as Mamacafé. Top-quality Mediterranean set meals are served here in a
modern, stylish environment. The ingredients
are bought fresh every day from the nearby
Mercat de la Boqueria. Enjoy Mamacafé's
excellent hamburgers and Tarte Tatin in the
company of its young and trendy patrons.

An Restaurants herrscht im hippen Raval
wahrlich kein Mangel – doch nicht alle sind
so empfehlenswert wie das Mamacafé. In
modern-stylischem Ambiente werden hier
mediterrane Menüs von zuverlässig guter
Qualität serviert – die täglich frisch ge-
kauften Zutaten stammen vom nahen
Mercat de la Boqueria. Der Hamburger
und die Tarte Tatin sind hervorragend, die
Gäste jung und trendy.

Raval est ultra-chic, et ce ne sont pas les
restaurants qui manquent – mais ils ne
sont pas tous à la hauteur du Mamacafé.
On sert ici dans une ambiance moderne
des menus méditerranéens de qualité –
les produits frais sont achetés tous les
jours au Mercat de la Boqueria tout proche. Le hamburger et la tarte Tatin sont
excellents, le public jeune et tendance.

3   Cooks' apparel/Gastronomie-
    bekleidung/Vêtements de cuisine

Sastrería El Transwaal
Carrer de l'Hospital 67
08001 Barcelona
Tel: +34 93 318 65 94
Mon–Fri 9.30am–1.30pm and 4.30pm–
8pm, Sat 9.30am–1.30pm
Metro: L3 Liceu

This shop sells professional apparel for the
food industry. It was considered extremely
modern when it opened in 1888. Anyone
who comes here – from sous-chef to sushi
chef, room-service waiter to chamber maid
– can still find a classic, custom-tailored
work outfit. A professional cook's apron
in blue cotton makes a very nice souvenir.
Even if you're only a home cook, this shop
will inspire you to ditch your flowered
aprons for something more professional
and stylish.

Dieser Laden führt Berufsbekleidung für

die Gastronomie. Er wurde 1888 eröffnet
und galt damals als äußerst modern. Noch
heute bekommt hier jeder – vom Souschef
bis zum Sushi-Chef, vom Etagenkellner bis
zum Zimmermädchen – ein klassisches Ar-
beitsoutfit nach individuellen Wünschen auf
den Leib geschneidert. Eine professionelle
Kochschürze aus blauem Baumwollzwirn
ist ein schönes Mitbringsel, denn damit
macht man am Herd einfach eine bessere
Figur als im geblümten Hausfrauenkittel.

Ce magasin spécialisé dans les vêtements
professionnels de cuisine a été ouvert en
1888 et, à l'époque, il était considéré comme extrêmement moderne. Aujourd'hui
encore, du sous-chef au chef sushi, du
garçon d'étage à la femme de chambre,
tous peuvent s'habiller classique et sur
mesure pour travailler. On peut rapporter
chez soi un tablier de cuisinier en fil de
coton bleu – quand on est aux fourneaux,
cela a quand même plus de classe qu'une
blouse à fleurs.

4   Market hall/Markthalle/Halle de marché

Mercat de la Boqueria
Plaça de la Boqueria
La Rambla 85-89
08001 Barcelona
Tel: +34 93 318 25 84
www.boqueria.info
Mon–Sat 8am–8.30pm
Metro: L3 Liceu; L1, L3 Catalunya

There are a handful of must-sees for any
first-time visitors to Barcelona: the Sagrada
Família, the Picasso Museum, the Santa
Maria del Mar church – and the Mercat de
la Boqueria. This market, with its 332
stalls, is often called the "stomach of
Barcelona", and it's still the best place in
town to buy fresh groceries. However, be
sure to shop there like a local, and head
for the back of the market, away from La
Rambla. That's where you'll find the less
touristy stalls, where you can buy all the
goodies you need (cold meats, cheese,
bread and fruit) for a picnic in the nearby
university gardens (see p. 50).

Wer zum ersten Mal nach Barcelona
kommt, muss die Sagrada Família, das

4   5

Museu Picasso, die Kirche Santa Maria del Mar und den Mercat de la Boqueria besuchen. Dieser Markt mit 332 Ständen wird auch der „Bauch von Barcelona" genannt und ist nach wie vor der beste Ort in der Stadt, um frische Lebensmittel einzukaufen. Man sollte es allerdings wie die Einheimischen machen und nach hinten durchgehen, weg von der Rambla. Dann entdeckt man die weniger touristischen Stände und findet alle Leckereien, die z. B. für ein Picknick in den nahen Universitätsgärten (siehe Seite 50) nötig sind: Salami, Käse, Brot und Früchte.

Celui qui se trouve pour la première fois à Barcelone doit visiter la Sagrada Família, le Museu Picasso, l'église Santa Maria del Mar et le Mercat de la Boqueria. Avec ses 332 étals, « le ventre de Barcelone » est, aujourd'hui comme hier, la meilleure adresse pour acheter des produits frais. Mais il faut imiter les habitants et aller au fond, loin de La Rambla, où se trouvent les étals moins touristiques. On peut y acheter tout ce qu'il faut – saucisson, fromage, pain et fruits – pour pique-niquer dans les jardins de l'Université (cf. p. 50) tout proches.

5   Suizos & churros/Suizos & Churros/ Suizos & churros

Granja La Pallaresa
Carrer de Petritxol 11
08001 Barcelona
Tel: +34 93 302 20 36
Daily from 9am–1pm and 4pm–9pm
Metro: L1, L3 Catalunya; L3 Liceu

You cannot leave Barcelona without trying "suizo", a hot drink that's like a liquid chocolate dessert, topped with a huge dollop of whipped cream. Better forget about that diet – this culinary delight is accompanied by deep-fried "churros" to dip into the hot chocolate. (Don't worry, nobody in Barcelona eats supper before 10pm, so you are bound to be hungry again later.) Besides Granja La Pallaresa, Granja Dulcinea and Granja M. Viader are considered the top spots to enjoy "suizo y churros" in the city.

Man darf Barcelona auf keinen Fall verlassen, ohne einen „suizo" getrunken zu

haben – ein heißes Getränk, das an einen flüssigen Schokoladenpudding erinnert und von einem Matterhorn Schlagsahne gekrönt wird. Jedweder Diätgedanke gehört sofort verbannt, denn zum Genuss gehören auch noch in Fett ausgebackene „churros" zum Eintunken in den Kakao (keine Sorge, in Barcelona wird nicht vor 22 Uhr zu Abend gegessen, so hat man später sicher wieder Hunger). Neben der Granja La Pallaresa gehören die Granja Dulcinea und die Granja M. Viader (siehe Seite 50) zu den Kultläden der Stadt.

Pas question de quitter Barcelone sans avoir dégusté un suizo. Un suizo c'est un chocolat chaud, épais et crémeux, surmonté d'une couronne de chantilly. Inutile de penser à votre ligne car ce plaisir suave est accompagné de churros frits que l'on peut tremper dans son chocolat (ne craignez pas de vous couper l'appétit : à Barcelone on ne dîne pas avant 22 h, et vous aurez sans doute une petite faim plus tard). À côté de la Granja La Pallaresa, la Granja Dulcinea et la Granja M. Viader (cf. p. 50) font partie des boutiques culte de la ville.

Personal discoveries/Eigene Entdeckungen/Découvertes personnelles :

Hostería Grau

Carrer de les Ramelleres, 27   08001 Barcelona
☎ +34 93 301 81 35   📠 +34 93 317 68 25
reservas@hostalgrau.com
www.hostalgrau.com
Metro: L1, L3 Catalunya
Booking: www.great-escapes-hotels.com

Hostería Grau

Barcelona has been designer-crazy since the city hosted the 1992 Olympics. But sometimes you get bored with thoroughly stylish hotels and yearn for the traditional Catalan style of a place like the Hostería Grau. This charming hotel for travellers on a shoestring is right in the middle of the Ciutat Vella, next to the Bar Cèntric, a meeting place for writers since 1862. Hostería guests are served breakfast in this atmospheric bar, a popular location for commercials, films and video clips (Dolce & Gabbana, for example). Although the hotel rooms range from the small to the Lilliputian, they all have a Mediterranean flair, thanks to the ceiling beams and terracotta floors. The proprietors tried to maintain the pleasant original ambience while renovating, and furnished all the rooms with a personal touch. The service is familial and friendly – you'll feel very well looked after, indeed.

Seit den Olympischen Spielen 1992 befindet sich Barcelona im Designfieber; doch manchmal hat man einfach genug von durchgestylten Hotels und sehnt sich nach traditionellem katalanischem Stil. Wie in der Hostería Grau: Das charmante Hotel fürs kleine Budget steht mitten in der Ciutat Vella neben der Bar Cèntric, die 1862 eröffnet und schnell zum Treffpunkt der Literaten wurde. Die Bar hat noch heute ein so authentisches Ambiente, dass hier schon Werbespots, Filme und Videoclips gedreht wurden (beispielsweise für Dolce & Gabbana) – Gästen der Hostería steht sie morgens zum Frühstück zur Verfügung. Die Hotelzimmer sind klein, zum Teil sogar winzig – sie besitzen aber dank alter Deckenbalken und Terrakottaböden mediterranes Flair. Bei der Renovierung haben sich die Besitzer bemüht, die angenehme Atmosphäre zu erhalten und alle Räume liebevoll einzurichten. Auch der Service ist familiär und freundlich, man fühlt sich hier rundum wohl.

La fièvre du design a gagné Barcelone depuis les Jeux Olympiques de 1992. Mais après tous ces hôtels peaufinés on se languit parfois de style catalan traditionnel. Je propose l'Hosteria Grau, un charmant établissement pour petits budgets situé au milieu de la Ciutat Vella à côté du Bar Cèntric. Ouvert en 1862, celui-ci est rapidement devenu le rendez-vous des gens de lettres et il est resté si authentique qu'on y a tourné des spots publicitaires, des films et des clips vidéo (par exemple pour Dolce & Gabbana) – le matin, les clients de l'hosteria peuvent y prendre leur petit déjeuner. Les chambres d'hôtel sont petites, parfois minuscules, mais on retrouve tout l'esprit méridional dans leurs vieilles poutres de plafond et leurs carrelages en brique. En rénovant les lieux, les propriétaires se sont efforcés de conserver l'atmosphère agréable et d'aménager toutes les pièces avec amour. Le service est aimable et liant – ici on se sent parfaitement bien.

Rates: Single rooms from 33 €, double rooms from 50 €, apartments from 75 €. Breakfast à la carte 2.80 €–7.50 €.
Rooms: 25 rooms and apartments (not all with en-suite bathrooms).
Cuisine: No in-house restaurant, but many restaurants in the immediate vicinity.
History: Founded in 1941, renovated in 2006.
X-Factor: Incredibly good location.
Internet: Access to a PC in the communal lounge (free of charge, high-speed).

Preise: EZ ab 33 €, DZ ab 50 €, Apartment ab 75 €. Frühstück à la carte 2,80–7,50 €.
Zimmer: 25 Zimmer und Apartments (nicht alle mit eigenem Bad).
Küche: Das Hotel besitzt kein Restaurant, in der unmittelbaren Umgebung gibt es aber zahlreiche Lokale.
Geschichte: 1941 gegründet und 2006 renoviert.
X-Faktor: Die unschlagbar gute Lage.
Internet: Im gemeinsamen Wohnzimmer steht ein Computer zur Verfügung (kostenfrei, highspeed).

Prix : Chambre simple à partir de 33 €, double à partir de 50 €, appartement à partir de 75 €. Petit déjeuner à la carte 2,80–7,50 €.
Chambres : 25 chambres et appartements (pas tous avec salle de bains).
Restauration : Pas de restaurant dans l'hôtel, mais de nombreux restaurants à proximité.
Histoire : Ouvert en 1941 et rénové en 2006.
Le « petit plus » : Sa situation unique.
Internet : Un ordinateur est à la disposition des clients dans le salon commun (gratuit, haut débit).

BOCADILLOS CALIENTES
SANDWICH'S AL GUSTO
DESAYUNOS
"BREAKFAST" "PRIMA COLAZIONE"
"PETIT DEJEUNER" FRÜHSTÜCK
"BUFFET FROID"

1

2

3

1 Oasis/Oase/Oasis

Jardins de la Universitat
Universitat de Barcelona
Gran Via de les Corts Catalanes 585
08007 Barcelona
Tel: +34 93 403 54 17
www.ub.es
Metro: L1, L2 Universitat

If you want to escape the noisy traffic at the Plaça de Catalunya, Avinguda Diagonal or La Rambla, then I recommend the delightful university gardens with their babbling fountains and tropical plants. You can sit on a bench with a thermos of coffee and a good book, like Luis Buñuel's *My Last Sigh*, and let the afternoon drift by. It's especially idyllic at the weekends, when the students stay at home and only the back entrance is open (Carrer de la Diputació).

Wer dem lärmenden Verkehr an der Plaça de Catalunya, Avinguda Diagonal oder der Rambla entgehen möchte, dem empfehle ich die zauberhaften Universitätsgärten mit plätschernden Brunnen und tropischen Pflanzen. Hier kann man sich mit einem Becher Kaffee und einem guten Buch wie Luis Buñuels „Mein letzter Seufzer" auf eine der Bänke setzen und den Nachmittag in aller Ruhe verstreichen lassen. Am Wochenende, wenn die Studenten zu Hause bleiben, ist nur der Hintereingang geöffnet (Carrer de la Diputació), dann ist es hier besonders idyllisch.

Pour échapper à la circulation bruyante sur la Plaça de Catalunya, Avinguda Diagonal ou La Rambla, je conseille les jardins enchanteurs de l'Université avec leurs fontaines gazouillantes et leurs plantes tropicales. Ici on peut s'asseoir sur un banc avec un gobelet de café et un bon livre, par exemple « Mon dernier soupir » de Luis Buñuel, et laisser l'après-midi s'écouler sereinement. Le week-end, quand les étudiants restent chez eux, il faut emprunter l'entrée de derrière (Carrer de la Diputació), mais l'endroit est alors idyllique.

2 Cocoa & milk bar/Kakao- & Milchbar/ Bar à lait & cacao

Granja M. Viader
Carrer d'en Xuclà 4-6
08001 Barcelona
Tel: +34 93 318 34 86
Mon 5pm–8.45pm, Tues–Sat 9am–1.45pm
and 5pm–8.45pm
Metro: L3 Liceu; L1, L3 Catalunya

It was in this "granja", a typical Catalan milk bar established in 1870, that the cocoa drink "Cacaolat" was invented. It is still on the menu today and has been served for many decades by waiters in smart white jackets and black bow ties. Besides "cacaolat", there are more than 20 different kinds of blended drinks, from banana shakes to the Barcelona favourite, "orxata", a milky drink made from tiger nuts. Another speciality you must try is "mel i mató", made of cream cheese with honey. The Granja is a popular stop for families, who pop in with their children after school in the afternoon.

In dieser 1870 eröffneten Granja, einer typisch katalanischen Milchbar, wurde 1931 der Kakao „Cacaolat" erfunden – er steht bis heute auf der Karte und wird von den seit Jahrzehnten gleichen Kellnern in weißen Jacken und mit schwarzen Fliegen serviert. Daneben gibt es mehr als 20 weitere Sorten an Mixgetränken, vom Bananenshake bis zur „orxata", einem milchigen Drink aus Erdmandeln, nach dem ganz Barcelona verrückt ist. Unbedingt versuchen sollte man auch eine weitere Spezialität: „mel i mató", Frischkäse mit Honig. Die Granja ist ein beliebter Zwischenstopp für Familien, die nachmittags mit ihren Kindern nach der Schule vorbeischauen.

C'est dans cette granja typiquement catalane inaugurée en 1870 qu'a été inventé en 1931 le chocolat au lait « Cacaolat ». Il est encore sur la carte et est servi depuis des décennies par des serveurs en veste blanche et nœud papillon noir. Mais on peut aussi déguster plus de vingt autres boissons, du milk-shake banane à l'« orxata », un orgeat de souchet dont les

Barcelonais raffolent. Il faut absolument goûter une autre spécialité le « mel i mató », un fromage frais au miel. La Granja est un endroit apprécié des familles qui y viennent l'après-midi avec leurs enfants après l'école.

3 Haberdashery & interior/Kurzwaren & Interieur/Mercerie & intérieur

Curtidos Pinós
Carrer de l'Hospital 79
08001 Barcelona
Tel: +34 93 317 63 84
www.curtidospinos.com
Mon–Fri 9am–2pm and 4pm–8pm,
Sat 9am–2pm
Metro: L3 Liceu

Traditional 19th-century haberdasheries like this one have all but vanished. It is amazing how many different kinds of yarn, borders, ribbons and threads are for sale here. And what a dizzying variety of materials, from linen, cotton and leather, to rubber and pvc! Take your time browsing through this shop with its beautiful interior. You're bound to find something useful, like a classy leather band for a pendant.

Solche traditionellen Kurzwarenläden aus dem 19. Jahrhundert existieren heute eigentlich gar nicht mehr. Es ist kaum zu glauben, wie viele Sorten an Garnen, Bordüren, Bändern und Fäden es aus wie vielen Materialien, wie Leinen, Leder, Kautschuk, PVC oder Baumwolle, gibt! Wer dieses Geschäft mit wunderschönem altem Holzinterieur besucht, braucht Zeit zum Stöbern – und findet bestimmt ein schickes Lederband für einen Anhänger; das kann man immer gut gebrauchen.

De telles merceries traditionnelles du XIXe siècle n'existent plus aujourd'hui. Et le choix immense de fils à coudre, de bordures et de rubans en lin, en cuir, en caoutchouc en PVC ou en coton laisse muet d'étonnement. Il faut prendre son temps pour farfouiller dans ce magasin superbement décoré à l'ancienne en bois – on y trouvera sûrement quelque chose d'utile, par exemple un ruban de cuir pour y fixer un pendentif.

4

5

6

---

4   Bakery/Bäckerei/Boulangerie

Barcelona Reykjavík

Carrer del Doctor Dou 12
08001 Barcelona
Tel: +34 93 302 09 21
www.barcelonareykjavik.com
Mon–Fri 10am–9pm, Sat 10am–4pm
Metro: L3 Liceu; L1, L2 Catalunya

This bakery smells fantastic and everything looks absolutely delicious. If you're
interested, you can go in the back of the
shop and watch how cakes, biscuits and
loaves of bread are baked with biodynamic
ingredients and without artificial additives.
The only disadvantage is that you usually
have to queue up to buy one of the luscious little "pastissos". There's a good
reason why this bakery is so popular!

Diese Bäckerei duftet herrlich und ist ein
äußerst appetitlicher Anblick. Neugierige
Kunden können hier auch beobachten, wie
im hinteren Teil des Ladens Kuchen, Kekse
und Brote aus biologisch-dynamischen
Zutaten und ohne künstliche Zusatzstoffe
hergestellt werden. Der einzige Nachteil
ist, dass man Schlange stehen muss, um
einen der köstlichen kleinen „pastissos"
zu erstehen – das Geschäft ist nicht ohne
Grund sehr beliebt.

L'odeur est exquise et l'aspect des produits on ne peut plus appétissant. Les
curieux peuvent regarder au fond du
magasin où l'on fait des gâteaux, des
gâteaux secs et du pain à l'aide d'ingrédients biologiques-dynamiques et sans
additifs artificiels. Le seul problème est
qu'il faut faire la queue pour acheter un
des savoureux petits « pastissos » – le
magasin est très apprécié et pour cause.

---

5   Garden café/Gartencafé/Café-jardin

El Jardí

Carrer de l'Hospital 56
08002 Barcelona
Tel: +34 93 329 15 50
Daily 10am–10.30pm (outside, but until
11pm inside)
Metro: L3 Liceu

Barcelona doesn't have many peaceful
oases. Either you're walking along one of
the large noisy boulevards, or wandering
in one of the busy little alleys in the Raval,
Barri Gòtic or Born districts. When you
need a break, head for this café, tucked
away in an inner courtyard. Here you can
enjoy a "cortado", a small coffee with a little
milk, while gazing up at the palm leaves,
or just looking at nothing in particular.

Es gibt nicht viele Oasen der Ruhe in
Barcelona – entweder befindet man sich
auf einem der großen Boulevards oder in
einer der belebten, engen Gassen der
Viertel Raval, Barri Gòtic oder Born. Wer
eine kleine Verschnaufpause benötigt,
sollte dieses Café besuchen, das sich in
einem Innenhof versteckt, und bei einem
„cortado" in die Palmenblätter oder einfach
in die Luft schauen.

Les oasis de paix sont rares à Barcelone
– soit on se trouve sur l'un des grands
boulevards, soit dans l'une des ruelles
animées des quartiers Raval, Barri Gòtic
ou Born. Celui qui veut se reposer un moment devrait entrer dans ce café dissimulé
dans une cour intérieure et contempler les
feuilles de palmier, ou le ciel tout simplement, en sirotant un petit « cortado ».

---

6   Sports club & swimming pool/
    Sportclub & Schwimmbad/
    Club sportif & Piscine

Club Natació Atlètic-Barceloneta

Plaça del Mar
08003 Barcelona
Tel: +34 93 221 00 10
www.cnab.org
Opening times depending on choice
of course.
Metro: L4 Barceloneta

If you think that you haven't used up
enough calories sightseeing, then you can
sweat off those "churros" in this sports
club right on the coast. The club offers
courses ranging from aqua gymnastics, to
water polo and spinning, to Tai Chi. The
club is members-only, but with a bit of
charm you may be able to negotiate your
way to a free trial class.

Wer beim Sightseeing noch nicht genug
Kalorien verbrannt hat, kann sich in diesem
Sportclub direkt am Meer richtig austoben.
Hier werden Kurse für jeden Geschmack
angeboten – von Aqua-Gymnastik über
Wasserball und Spinning bis hin zum Tai-Chi.
Eigentlich haben hier nur Mitglieder Zutritt,
mit etwas Verhandlungsgeschick lässt sich
aber eine Probestunde arrangieren.

Si vous n'avez pas encore brûlé assez
de calories en visitant la ville, vous pouvez
vous défouler dans ce club sportif situé
en bord de mer. Ici, il y en a pour tous les
goûts – de la gymnastique aquatique au
tai chi, en passant par le waterball et le
spinning. En principe seuls les membres
du club y ont accès, mais avec un peu
d'adresse vous réussirez à soutirer une
heure d'essai.

Personal discoveries/Eigene
Entdeckungen/Découvertes personnelles :

_____

_____

_____

_____

_____

_____

_____

_____

_____

_____

_____

_____

Hotel Pulitzer

Carrer de Bergara, 8   08002 Barcelona
☎ +34 93 481 67 67   ☐ +34 93 481 64 64
info@hotelpulitzer.es
www.hotelpulitzer.es
Metro: L1, L3 Catalunya
Booking: www.great-escapes-hotels.com

Hotel Pulitzer

Hotel Pulitzer is located on a side street that leads to Plaça de Catalunya, within walking distance of the tourist attractions in the Eixample and El Raval districts. The reception desk in the lobby is made out of a baroque Sicilian altar with gilded carvings. Lázaro Rosa Violán decorated the building with stylish modern taste, creating just the right ambience for the sophisticated urban traveller. White leather sofas and armchairs dominate the lobby, and a potentially severe colour palette of white, black and gold is softened by the careful use of wood. The elegant rooms boast wooden floors, leather sofas and chocolate-coloured armchairs. There is also a library (with a lot of TASCHEN books), a restaurant (Visit), a bar and a roof garden, all of which will tempt guests to linger in the hotel, rather than explore the city. This is a hip place indeed, but it would be even better if the staff were friendlier.

Das Hotel Pulitzer liegt in einer Seitenstraße, die auf die Plaça de Catalunya führt, und in Fußnähe der Sehenswürdigkeiten der Viertel Eixample und Raval. Empfangen wird man an einer einzigartigen Rezeption, die aus einem sizilianischen Barockaltar mit goldenen Schnitzereien gefertigt wurde. Für das Design war Lázaro Rosa Violán verantwortlich, der das Haus absolut stilvoll-modern ausgestattet hat – ganz dem Geschmack eines weit gereisten Großstädters entsprechend. In der Lobby dominieren weiße Ledersofas und -sessel, aufgelockert wird das Ensemble aus Weiß, Schwarz und Gold von Holztönen. Die Zimmer sind sehr elegant mit Holzböden, Ledersofas und schokoladefarbenen Sesseln eingerichtet. Es gibt eine Bücherei mit vielen Titeln von TASCHEN, das Restaurant Visit, eine Bar und einen Dachgarten – all das verführt fast dazu, im Hotel zu bleiben, anstatt die City zu erkunden. Eine angesagte Adresse, nur das Personal könnte freundlicher sein.

Situé dans une rue latérale qui mène à la Plaça de Catalunya, l'hôtel Pulitzer se dresse à quelque pas des curiosités des quartiers L'Eixample et El Raval. À la réception, le client se retrouve devant un autel baroque sicilien aux sculptures dorées, unique en son genre. Lázaro Rosa Violán, responsable du design a décoré les lieux avec un grand souci d'élégance et de modernité – ce qui correspond tout à fait au goût de l'habitant de la grande ville venu de loin. Dans le hall dominent les canapés et fauteuils de cuir blanc. L'ensemble blanc, noir et or est assoupli par des tons de bois. Les chambres dotées de parquets abritent des canapés de cuir et des fauteuils couleur chocolat. La bibliothèque qui offre de nombreux titres de TASCHEN, le restaurant Visit, le bar et le toit en terrasse donnent envie de rester à l'hôtel au lieu de visiter la ville. Une adresse à retenir ; mais le personnel pourrait être plus aimable.

Rates: Single rooms from 165 €, double rooms from 190 €, suites from 520 €, including breakfast.
Rooms: 91 rooms and suites.
Cuisine: The stylish restaurant with its idyllic patio offers Mediterranean meals with an Asian touch. There is also a cocktail bar and a pool bar on the roof terrace.
History: Opened in 2004.
X-Factor: Active holidaymakers can visit the nearby fitness club, Holmes Place.
Internet: Free of charge (high-speed, WLAN).

Preise: EZ ab 165 €, DZ ab 190 €, Suite ab 520 €; inklusive Frühstück.
Zimmer: 91 Zimmer und Suiten.
Küche: Das schicke Restaurant mit idyllischem Patio bietet mediterrane Menüs, die mit orientalischen Aromen verfeinert sind. Zudem gibt es eine Cocktailbar und eine Poolbar auf der Dachterrasse.
Geschichte: 2004 eröffnet.
X-Faktor: Aktivurlaubern steht der nahe Fitnessclub Holmes Place offen.
Internet: Kostenfrei (highspeed, WLAN).

Prix : Chambre simple à partir de 165 €, double à partir de 190 €, suite à partir de 520 € ; petit déjeuner inclus.
Chambres : 91 chambres et suites.
Restauration : Le restaurant chic au patio idyllique sert des plats méditerranéens aux parfums d'Orient. Bar à cocktails et pool-bar sur le toit-terrasse.
Histoire : Ouvert en 2004.
Le « petit plus » : Le club de remise en forme « Holmes Place » tout proche est ouvert aux adeptes des vacances actives.
Internet : Gratuit (haut débit, WLAN).

1   Catalan architecture & interior/
    Katalanische Architektur & Interieur/
    Architecture catalane & intérieur

Hotel España
Carrer de Sant Pau 9-11
08001 Barcelona
Tel: +34 93 318 17 58
www.hotelespanya.com
Metro: L3 Liceu

This architectural gem was built in 1902 by leading Catalan architect Lluís Domènech i Montaner. Except for a few cheap vending machines in the lobby, the hotel bears no traces of the masses of tourists who are herded through. Even if it is impossible to spend a night in the hotel because of the package tours, you should at least have a drink here, and admire the impressive décor – which includes colourful tiles, wooden carvings, a five-metre-high fireplace and huge frescoes depicting sea creatures.

Der bedeutende katalanische Architekt Lluís Domènech i Montaner hat dieses architektonische Juwel 1902 erbaut. Bis auf ein paar billige Getränkeautomaten in der Lobby hat das Hotel die Touristen-massen, die hier durchgeschleust werden, glücklicherweise unbeschadet überstanden. Auch wenn man wegen der Pauschalrei-senden hier nicht übernachten kann, so sollte man in dem überwältigenden Dekor mit bunten Fliesen, einem fünf Meter hohen Kamin, riesigen Fresken mit Meeresgestalten und Holzschnitzereien wenigstens ein Bier trinken.

Le célèbre architecte catalan Lluís Domènech i Montaner a construit cette merveille en 1902. Si l'on néglige les quelques distributeurs de boissons bon marché dans le hall, on peut dire que l'hôtel a heureusement résisté aux légions de touristes. Même si on ne peut pas passer la nuit ici à cause des voyageurs à forfait, il faut au moins boire une bière dans ce décor sublime qui offre des carrelages multicolores, une cheminée de cinq mètres de haut, des fresques gigan-tesques avec des créatures marines et des bois sculptés.

2   Market bar/Marktbar/Bar du marché

Bar Pinotxo
Mercat de la Boqueria
Plaça de la Boqueria
La Rambla 85-89
08001 Barcelona
Tel: +34 93 317 17 31
Mon–Sat 5.30am–5pm
Metro: L3 Liceu

The tiny Pinotxo Bar (Pinocchio Bar) is located on the premises of the Boqueria market, very close to the entrance on La Rambla side. It has been an institution since it opened. Some of the barmen have been standing behind the small bar in their dark trousers and white shirts for more than 50 years, serving guests at top speed. It's best to drink your "cortado" here in the early morning, elbow to elbow with Barcelona chefs getting ready to snap up the crispest vegetables and the freshest fish in the market.

Die winzige Bar Pinotxo („Pinocchio") liegt auf dem Gelände des Boqueria-Marktes, ganz nahe am Eingang von der Rambla. Seit ihrer Eröffnung ist sie eine Institution – einige Barmänner stehen bereits seit mehr als 50 Jahren in dunkler Hose und weißem Hemd hinter der übersichtlichen Theke und bedienen ihre Gäste in Höchst-geschwindigkeit. Am besten trinkt man hier frühmorgens seinen „cortado" Schulter an Schulter mit den Küchenchefs, die an-schließend auf dem Markt das knackigste Gemüse und den frischesten Fisch ergat-tern möchten.

Le minuscule Pinotxo (« Pinocchio ») est situé sur le marché de la Boqueria, juste à l'entrée, près de La Rambla. Il est une in-stitution depuis qu'il est ouvert – certains barmans en pantalon foncé et chemise blanche sont derrière le comptoir depuis plus d'un demi-siècle et servent les clients à une vitesse record. Le mieux est de boire ici son « cortado » tôt le matin en compagnie des cuisiniers qui vont se rendre au marché pour acheter les plus beaux légumes et le poisson le plus frais.

3   Coffee roasters/Kaffeerösterei/
    Torréfaction

La Portorriqueña
Carrer d'en Xuclà 25
08001 Barcelona
Tel: +34 93 317 34 38
Mon–Sat 9am–2pm and 5pm–8pm
Metro: L1, L3 Catalunya

Coffee is the national beverage of Spain, just as it is in Italy. In fact, you can find even more shops here that roast the beans just before selling. The aroma is amazing! If you are looking for a souvenir, I recom-mend buying some of the house blend at La Portorriqueña, founded in 1902. The coffee is sold in the original, chic-looking packaging that was designed in the '70s.

Wie in Italien ist Kaffee auch in Spanien das Nationalgetränk Nummer eins – hier findet man sogar noch häufiger Läden, in denen die Bohnen kurz vor dem Verkauf frisch geröstet werden. Der Duft ist un-vergleichlich! Ich empfehle, in der 1902 gegründeten La Portorriqueña ein Paket der Hausmischung als Souvenir zu erste-hen; schon alleine wegen des schicken und originalen Verpackungsdesigns aus den 1970ern.

Comme en Italie, le café est la boisson nationale en Espagne. Ici on trouve même encore plus souvent des marchands qui torréfient eux-mêmes le café juste avant de le vendre. L'odeur est incomparable ! Je vous conseille d'acheter un paquet du mélange maison à La Portorriqueña fondée en 1902. Cela vous fera un beau souvenir rien qu'à cause du design années 1970 de l'emballage chic et original.

4   Pastry shop/Konditorei/Pâtisserie

Escribà
Rambla de les Flors 83
08002 Barcelona
Tel: +34 93 301 60 27
www.escriba.es
Daily 8.30am–9pm
Metro: L3 Liceu

4

5

On La Rambla, the beautiful "Modernismo" façade catches the eye like a sparkling gem: the violet and green mosaic with Art Nouveau lettering and coloured-glass windows is a real work of art. The historic building houses one of three branches of the pastry-shop empire Escribà, founded in 1906 in the Gran Via (in addition to the popular beach restaurant Xiringuito d'Escribà, Litoral Mar 42). The interior complements the style of the façade. Tea and luscious little cakes are served in this darling café – the Starbucks next door seems light years away.

Auf der Rambla sticht die wunderschöne Modernismo-Fassade wie ein funkelndes Juwel ins Auge – das violett-grüne Mosaik mit Jugendstilschrift und Buntglasfenstern ist ein echtes Kunstwerk. Das historische Gebäude gehört zu den drei Niederlassungen des 1906 an der Gran Via gegründeten Konditorei-Imperiums Escribà (dazu kommt das beliebte Strandrestaurant Xiringuito d'Escribà, Litoral Mar 42). Das Interieur führt den Stil der Fassade fort. Im hübschen Café werden Tee und köstliche Törtchen serviert – Lichtjahre entfernt vom Starbucks nebenan.

Sur La Rambla, la façade Modernismo attire le regard comme un bijou scintillant – la mosaïque violette et verte avec inscription Art nouveau et fenêtres en verre coloré est une véritable œuvre d'art. Le bâtiment historique abrite l'une des trois filiales de l'empire pâtissier Escribà, fondé en 1906 sur la Gran Via (s'y ajoute le restaurant de plage, le très populaire Xiringuito d'Escribà, Litoral Mar 42). L'intérieur tient les promesses de la façade ; dans le joli café on peut déguster du thé et de succulentes tartelettes – à des années-lumière du Starbucks voisin.

5   Café & bar/Café & Bar/Café & bar

Bar Lobo
Carrer del Pintor Fortuny 3
08001 Barcelona
Tel: +34 93 481 53 46
www.grupotragaluz.com
Daily from midday to midnight
Metro: L1, L3 Catalunya; L3 Liceu

This trendy tapas bar is managed by the Tragaluz group, which owns many of the best restaurants in Barcelona, as well as Hotel Omm. The bar is located right in the middle of the Raval, on the pleasant cross-roads of Carrer Pintor del Fortuny and Carrer d'en Xuclà. A crowd of mostly young people congregates here to enjoy the excellent tapas.

Diese trendige Tapas-Bar wird von der Tragaluz-Gruppe geführt, der in Barcelona zahlreiche der besten Restaurants sowie das Hotel Omm gehören. Sie liegt mitten im Raval an der idyllischen Ecke der Carrer Pintor del Fortuny und Carrer d'en Xuclà. Ein junges Publikum lässt sich hier ausgezeichnete Tapas schmecken.

Ce bar à tapas tendance appartient au groupe Tragaluz qui possède à Barcelone nombre des meilleurs restaurants ainsi que l'hôtel Omm. Il est situé en plein cœur du Raval au coin idyllique de la Carrer Pintor del Fortuny et de la Carrer d'en Xuclà. Il est le rendez-vous de la jeunesse qui apprécie les succulentes tapas.

Personal discoveries/Eigene Entdeckungen/Découvertes personnelles :

Barri Gòtic
La Ribera

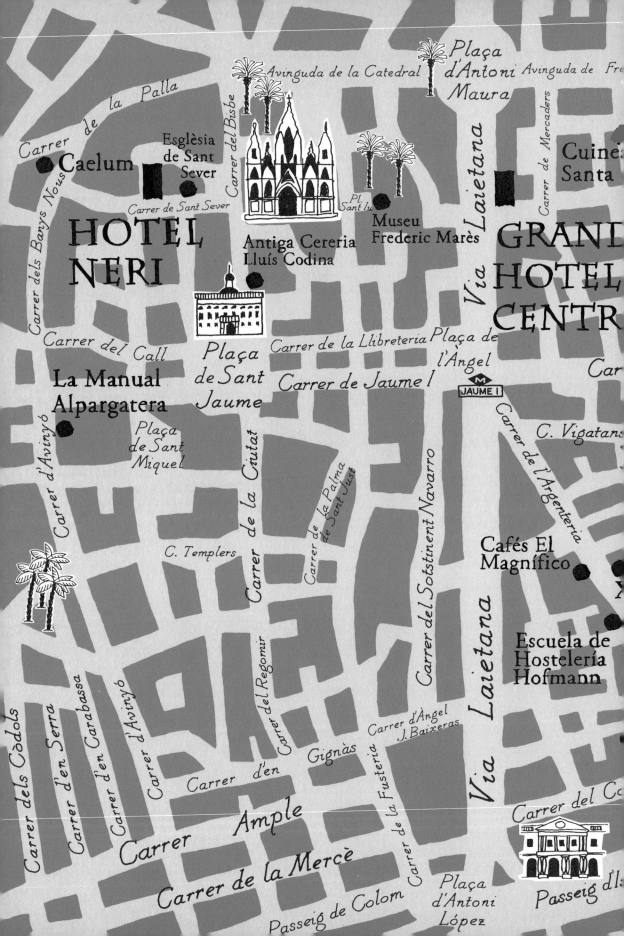

Carrer de la Palla

Carrer del Bisbe

Caelum

Esglèsia
de Sant
Sever

Avinguda de la Catedral

Plaça
d'Antoni
Maura

Avinguda de Fra

Carrer de Mercaders

Carrer de

Cuiné
Santa

Carrer de Sant Sever

HOTEL
NERI

Carrer dels Banys Nous

Pl.
Sant Iu

Antiga Cereria
Lluís Codina

Museu
Frederic Marès

Via Laietana

GRAND
HOTEL
CENTR

Carrer del Call

La Manual
Alpargatera

Carrer d'Avinyó

Plaça
de Sant
Jaume

Plaça
de Sant
Miquel

Carrer de la Llibreteria

Carrer de Jaume I

Plaça de
l'Àngel

JAUME I

Carrer de la Ciutat

Carrer de la Palma de Sant Just

C. Templers

Carrer del Regomir

Carrer del Sotstinent Navarro

Carrer de l'Argenteria

C. Vigatans

Cafés El
Magnífico

X

Escuela de
Hostelería
Hofmann

Carrer dels Còdols

Carrer d'en Serra

Carrer d'en Carabassa

Carrer d'Avinyó

Carrer d'en

Gignàs

Carrer d'Àngel
J. Baixeras

Carrer de la Fusteria

Carrer Ample

Carrer del Co

Via Laietana

Carrer de la Mercè

Passeig de Colom

Plaça
d'Antoni
López

Passeig d'Is

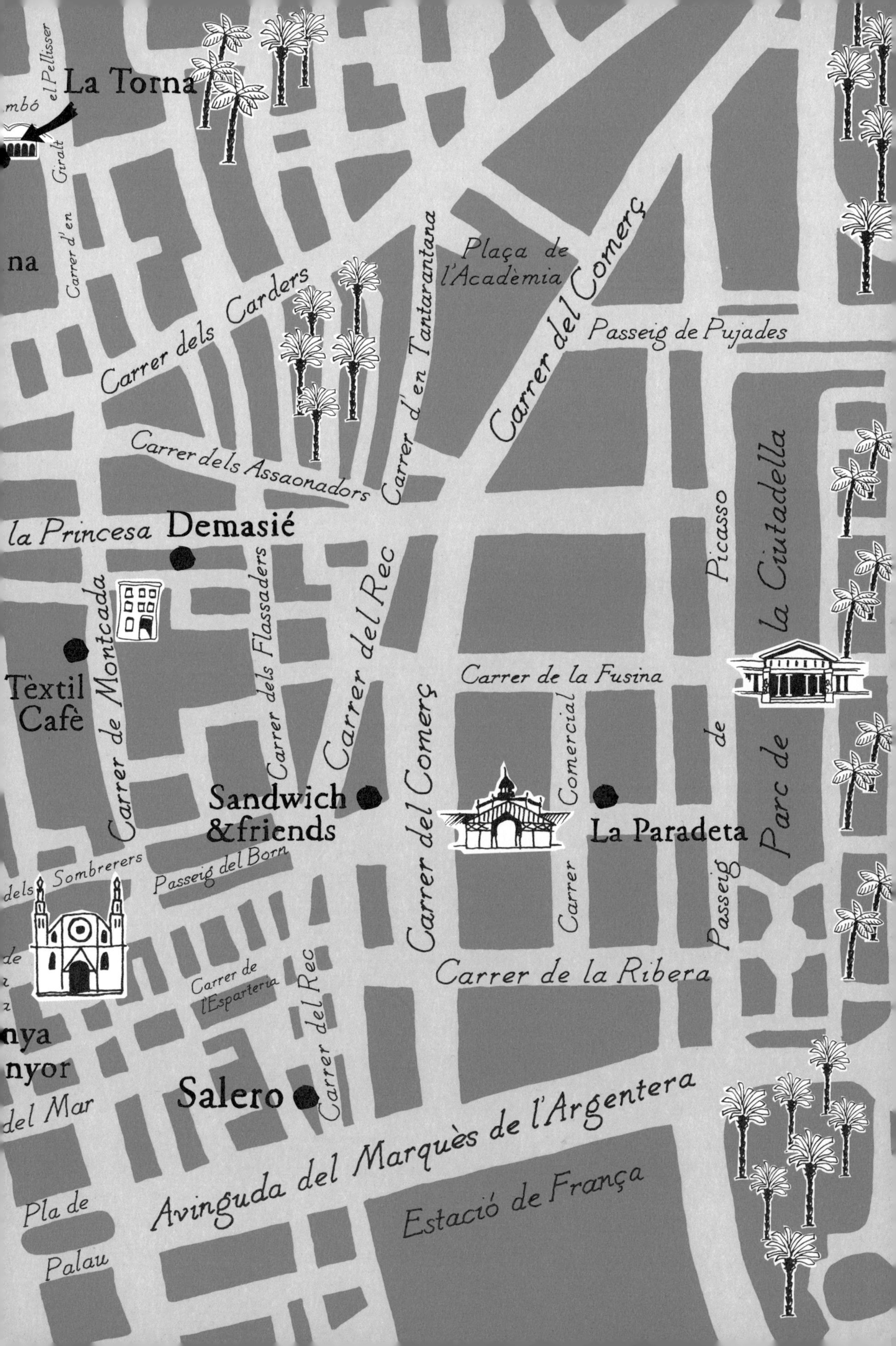

La Torna

mbó el Pellisser

Carrer d'en Giralt

na

Carrer dels Carders

Carrer d'en Tantantana

Plaça de l'Acadèmia

Carrer del Comerç

Passeig de Pujades

Carrer dels Assaonadors

la Princesa Demasié

Carrer de Montcada

Carrer dels Flassaders

Carrer del Rec

Tèxtil Cafè

Carrer de la Fusina

la Ciutadella

Picasso

Sandwich &friends

Carrer del Comerç

Carrer Comercial

La Paradeta

Parc de

dels Sombrerers

Passeig del Born

de

Passeig

Carrer del Rec

Carrer de la Ribera

nya nyor

Carrer de l'Esparteria

del Mar

Salero

Avinguda del Marquès de l'Argentera

Pla de

Estació de França

Palau

Hotel Neri

Carrer de Sant Sever, 5   08002 Barcelona
☎ +34 93 304 06 55   📠 +34 93 304 03 37
info@hotelneri.com
www.hotelneri.com
Metro: L4 Jaume I; L3 Liceu
Booking: www.great-escapes-hotels.com

Hotel Neri

This little gem is located on one of the most atmospheric squares I know, the Plaça de Sant Felip Neri. With its cobblestones, baroque church, fountain and gnarled old trees, this is an enchanted, other-worldly place, so try to book a room with a view of the Plaça. If that's not possible, don't worry – the hotel bar always puts out a few sidewalk tables, so you can drink in the atmosphere along with a glass of wine. Inside the hotel, Cristina Gabás's interior design is a treat for all the senses, and she cleverly blends old elements with the avant-garde. The range of subtle, subdued shades is punctuated by a splash of red here, a touch of gold-leaf there. The combination of unvarnished wood, chandeliers and shimmering velvet and taffeta provides a very ingenious contrast to the bare stone walls. The quartzite bathrooms are appointed with complimentary Etro products.

Dieses kleine Juwel liegt an einem der stimmungsvollsten Plätze, die ich je gesehen habe, der Plaça de Sant Felip Neri. Mit Kopfsteinpflaster, einer barocken Kirche, einem Springbrunnen, knorrigen Bäumen und nachts von ein paar Gaslaternen beschienen, ist dieser Ort magisch und nicht von dieser Welt. Deshalb sollte man versuchen, ein Zimmer mit Blick auf die Plaça zu reservieren, ansonsten stehen hier abends ein paar Tische der Hotelbar, sodass man die Atmosphäre bei einem Glas Wein genießen kann. Im Inneren des Hauses möchte das Design von Cristina Gabás alle Sinne ansprechen – und mischt geschickt alte Elemente mit avantgardistischen. Die Palette aus ruhigen dumpfen Tönen wird hier und da durch einen roten Farbtupfer oder Blattgold unterbrochen; der Material-Mix aus rohem Holz, changierendem Samt und Taft sowie Kristallleuchtern im Kontrast zu dem kargen Gemäuer ist äußerst raffiniert. In den Quarzit-Bädern liegen Produkte von Etro bereit.

Ce petit bijou est situé sur l'une des places les plus couleur locale que je connaisse, la Plaça de Sant Felip Neri. Avec ses pavés inégaux, son église baroque, sa fontaine, ses arbres tordus et ses réverbères qui l'éclairent la nuit, ce lieu est magique, tout simplement irréel. Vous avez donc tout intérêt à réserver une chambre donnant sur la Plaça. Mais vous pourrez aussi jouir le soir de de son atmosphère en vous asseyant avec un verre de vin aux tables du bar de l'hôtel. À l'intérieur, le design de Cristina Gabás interpelle tous les sens et marie avec bonheur l'ancien et l'avant-garde. Les couleurs mates sont interrompues ici et là par une touche d'or ou de rouge. Bois brut, satin et taffetas aux coloris chatoyants et chandeliers en cristal forment un contraste particulièrement raffiné avec la sobriété des murs. Des produits de la marque Etro sont à votre disposition dans les salles de bains tout en quartzite.

Rates: Single and double rooms from 295 €, junior suites from 360 €. Breakfast 25 €.
Rooms: 22 rooms and suites.
Cuisine: The restaurant specialises in Mediterranean dishes, many with interesting Arabian or medieval touches.
History: An 18th-century town mansion transformed into a very special hotel.
X-Factor: The roof terrace with a view over the district.
Internet: Free of charge (high-speed, WLAN).

Preise: EZ/DZ ab 295 €, Junior Suite ab 360 €. Frühstück 25 €.
Zimmer: 22 Zimmer und Suiten.
Küche: Das Restaurant hat sich auf mediterrane Gerichte spezialisiert – viele Rezepte haben interessante arabische oder mittelalterliche Einflüsse.
Geschichte: Aus einem Stadtpalais des 18. Jahrhunderts wurde ein atmosphärisches Designhotel.
X-Faktor: Die Dachterrasse mit Blick über das Viertel.
Internet: Kostenfrei (highspeed, WLAN).

Prix : Chambre simple ou double à partir de 295 €, Junior Suite à partir de 360 €. Petit-déjeuner 25 €.
Chambres : 22 chambres et suites.
Restauration : Le restaurant s'est spécialisé dans la cuisine méditerranéenne. Beaucoup de plats présentent une influence arabe ou moyenâgeuse intéressante.
Histoire : L'ancien hôtel particulier du XVIIIe siècle est devenu un hôtel design plein d'atmosphère.
Le « petit plus » : La terrasse sur le toit dominant le quartier.
Internet : Gratuit (haut débit, WLAN).

1

2

3

1 Fine fare from monasteries & tea salon/
Gutes aus Klöstern & Teesalon/
Délices monastiques & salon de thé

Caelum
Carrer de la Palla 8
08002 Barcelona
Tel: +34 93 302 69 93
Daily 10.30am–2pm and 5pm–9pm
Metro: L3 Liceu

This exceptional boutique-cum-tea salon
is heaven on earth. The little shop sells
products from 38 different monastery
communities in Spain. Here you'll find very
tasty liqueurs, marzipan cake, biscuits,
cheese, dark jam and all kinds of herb-
infused vinegar. They also sell candles
and bars of soap with pictures of angels.
All the products are beautifully wrapped
and make perfect little presents. In the
café, try the "alfajores", made with dried
fruit, nuts and honey, with your tea – out
of this world.

Diese einzigartige Boutique mit Teesalon
ist ein Himmel auf Erden. Der kleine Laden
verkauft Produkte von 38 Klostergemein-
schaften in Spanien: intensive Liköre,
Marzipankuchen, Kekse, dunkle Marmeladen
und mit Kräutern angesetzte Essigsorten.
Zudem gibt es Kerzen und Seifen mit
Engelsbildern – alle Einkäufe werden
wunderschön verpackt und sind somit
perfekt als Mitbringsel geeignet. Probieren
Sie im Café zum Tee den „alfajores" aus
getrockneten Früchten, Nüssen und Honig
und Sie wähnen sich im Paradies.

Cette boutique avec salon de thé est le
paradis sur terre. Le petit magasin vend
les produits de trente-huit monastères
espagnols : liqueurs enivrantes, gâteaux
au massepain, biscuits, confitures et
vinaigres aux herbes. Il propose par
ailleurs des bougies et des savons avec
des images d'anges. Vos achats sont si
joliment emballés que vous pourrez les
offrir de retour chez vous. Au salon de
thé, n'hésitez pas à goûter les « alfajores »,
ces succulents biscuits aux fruits secs, aux
noisettes et au miel. Absolument divin !

2 Restaurant & architecture/Restaurant
& Architektur/Restaurant & architecture

Cuines Santa Caterina
Mercat de Santa Caterina
Avinguda de Francesc Cambó 20
08003 Barcelona
Tel: +34 93 268 99 18
www.grupotragaluz.com
Daily 1pm–4pm and 8pm–midnight
Metro: L4 Jaume I

This excellent restaurant belongs to the
Mercat de Santa Caterina, which was built
by Enric Miralles. The Mercat is both a
successful reinterpretation of a 19th-cen-
tury market hall, and an homage to Gaudí.
Quality and freshness are the restaurant's
pride; the chef only uses foodstuffs that
come from the market. The menu is printed
on paper placemats and lists the dishes
by ingredient.

Dieses ausgezeichnete Restaurant gehört zu dem von Enric Miralles gebauten
Mercat de Santa Caterina, eine gelungene
Neuinterpretation der Markthallen des
19. Jahrhunderts und eine Hommage an
Gaudí. Frische sowie gute Qualität sind
hier garantiert, denn alle Lebensmittel,
die der Küchenchef verwendet, stammen
ausschließlich vom Markt selbst. Die Speisekarte ist auf dem Tischset aus Papier ge-
druckt und präsentiert die Gerichte
nach Zutaten geordnet.

Cet excellent restaurant est situé dans le
marché couvert Mercat de Santa Caterina,
construit par Enric Miralles dans le style
des halles du XIXe siècle et en hommage
à Gaudí. Vous pouvez être sûr de la fraî-
cheur et de la qualité des mets car le chef
utilise des produits achetés uniquement
sur le marché. La carte est inscrite sur le
set de table et les plats sont présentés
suivant leurs ingrédients.

3 Culinary school/Kochschule/École
hôtelière

Escuela de Hostelería Hofmann
Carrer de l'Argenteria 74-78
08003 Barcelona

Tel. +34 93 319 58 89
www.hofmann-bcn.com
Opening times depend on course schedule.
Metro: L4 Jaume I

The culinary school is directly opposite the
beautiful church of Santa Maria del Mar.
The students, in their white uniforms and
toques, often sit on the church steps to
relax in the sun after their classes. The
Escuela classrooms have a driving-school
feel to them. On the top floor there's a
restaurant where you can play guinea pig
for the up-and-coming generation of
young chefs.

Die Kochschule liegt direkt gegenüber der
wunderschönen Kirche Santa Maria del
Mar. Oft sitzen die Schüler in ihren weißen
Anzügen auf den Kirchenstufen, um sich
in der Sonne vom Unterricht zu erholen.
Der Klassenraum der Escuela verströmt
das Flair einer Fahrschule – in der oberen
Etage gibt es ein Restaurant, in dem man
als Versuchskaninchen der Nachwuchs-
köche dienen kann.

L'école hôtelière se trouve en face de
la très belle église Santa Maria del Mar.
Il n'est pas rare de voir des élèves en
uniforme blanc s'asseoir au soleil sur les
marches de l'église pour se détendre
après la classe. La salle de cours de
l'Escuela fait penser à une auto-école :
à l'étage supérieur, il y a un restaurant
dans lequel on peut servir de cobaye
aux cuisiniers en herbe.

4 Wine bar & tapas/Weinbar & Tapas/
Vins & tapas

La Vinya del Senyor
Plaça de Santa Maria 5
08003 Barcelona
Tel: +34 93 310 33 79
Tues–Sun midday–1am
Metro: L4 Jaume I

This small but top-rate and unpretentious
bar has an excellent selection of national
and international wine, as well as cava,
Catalan champagne. Typical Catalan tapas,
such as "bacallà amb tomàquet", are
served as an accompaniment to the wine.

4

5

A special pleasure: sitting with your wine and tapas at a table in the small square with an unobstructed view of the Gothic church of Santa Maria del Mar.

Eine kleine, aber sehr feine und zugleich unprätentiöse Bar. Sie bietet eine hervorragende Auswahl an nationalen und internationalen Weinen sowie „cava", katalanischen Champagner. Dazu werden typisch katalanische Tapas wie „bacallà amb tomàquet" serviert. Besonders schön sind die Tische auf dem kleinen Platz mit direktem Blick auf die gotische Kirche Santa Maria del Mar.

Un petit bar sans prétention mais qui offre un choix excellent de vins nationaux et internationaux ainsi que du « cava », le champagne catalan. On vous sert en accompagnement des tapas typiquement catalanes, comme les « bacallà amb tomàquet ». Les tables sur la petite place avec vue sur l'église gothique de Santa Maria del Mar sont particulièrement agréables.

5   Candles & devotional articles/Kerzen & Devotionalien/Cierges & objets de dévotion

Antiga Cereria Lluís Codina
Carrer del Bisbe 2
08002 Barcelona
Tel: +34 93 315 08 08
Mon–Sat 9am–1.30pm and 4.30pm–7.45pm, Sun 10am–1.30pm
Metro: L4 Jaume I

This is another one of Barcelona's delightful and unique little shops. Here in deeply religious Catholic Spain you can find very attractive devotional articles – christening or communion candles, rosaries, Madonna figurines and crucifixes. The interior dates back to the 19th century and feels like a film set. Another shop with a wide range of candles is Cereria Subirà, established in 1761, which is the oldest shop in Barcelona. It is just a step away, at Baixada de la Llibreteria 7.

Ein weiteres dieser wunderbaren kleinen Geschäfte in Barcelona, wie es sie sonst kaum noch gibt. Im tief religiösen, katholi-

schen Spanien findet man besonders schöne Devotionalien wie Tauf- oder Kommunionskerzen, Rosenkränze, Madonnenfiguren und Kreuze. Das Interieur stammt aus dem 19. Jahrhundert und könnte als Filmset eingesetzt werden. Ein großes Kerzensortiment bietet auch die nicht weit entfernte Cereria Subirà – sie eröffnete 1761 und ist damit der älteste Laden der Stadt (Baixada de la Llibreteria 7).

Un autre de ces merveilleux petits magasins comme il en existe à peine encore à Barcelone. Dans cette Espagne catholique, profondément religieuse, on trouve des objets de dévotion de toute beauté, comme des cierges de baptême et de communion, des chapelets, des Madone et des crucifix. Datant du XIXe siècle, la décoration intérieure pourrait servir de décor à un film. Non loin de là, le petit magasin Cereria Subirà offre lui aussi un grand choix de cierges. Ouvert en 1761, il est le plus vieux magasin de la ville (Baixada de la Llibreteria 7).

Personal discoveries/Eigene Entdeckungen/Découvertes personnelles :

6

7

8

6 Tea salon & interior/Teesalon & Interieur/Salon de thé & intérieur

Xador
Carrer de l'Argenteria 61-63
08003 Barcelona
Tel: +34 93 268 90 28
Daily 9am–midnight
Metro: L4 Jaume I

Visitors should be sure not to miss the beautiful, well-preserved Art Nouveau façade and the original interior of this tea salon. If only they didn't serve deep-freeze pizzas and micro-waved paella, this shop would be an absolute gem. Go there anyway, and order a "cerveza" – who knows how long the rest will survive?

Man sollte sich beim Besuch dieses Teesalons auf die wunderschöne, gut erhaltene Jugendstilfassade und das originale Interieur konzentrieren. Dieser Laden könnte ein Schmuckstück sein, aber leider werden hier Tiefkühlpizza und Mikrowellenpaella serviert. Trotzdem: Bestellen Sie eine „cerveza", denn wer weiß, wie lange sich der Rest noch halten wird.

Concentrez-vous ici sur la magnifique façade, de style art nouveau, parfaitement conservée et sur la décoration intérieure qui ne manque pas d'originalité. Pour ce qui est de la restauration, il est dommage qu'on y serve des pizzas congelées et des paellas réchauffées au micro-ondes. Commandez-y malgré tout une « cerveza », car qui sait pour combien de temps encore le décor va être gardé.

7 Sandwiches/Sandwiches/Sandwiches

Sandwich & friends
Passeig del Born 27
08003 Barcelona
Tel: +34 93 310 07 86
www.sandwichandfriends.com
Sun–Wed 9.30am–1am, Thurs–Sat 9.30am–2am
Metro: L4 Jaume I

This unassuming sandwich bar is in a pretty part of the picturesque Passeig del Born.

Cesc Pons designed the hip interior, which is stylishly accentuated by an oversized mural by internationally renowned illustrator Jordi Labanda. This is a good place for an informal, unfussy meal; you can get a good salad or a cold or hot sandwich here. Each of the 50 different freshly cut sandwiches on the menu is named after a friend of the owner's.

An einer schönen Stelle des malerischen Passeig del Born ist diese unprätentiöse Sandwich-Bar gelegen. Das coole Interieur wurde von Cesc Pons entworfen, und ein überdimensionales Wandgemälde des international bekannten Illustrators Jordi Labanda verleiht dem Ganzen eine stylische Note. Hier kann man ohne großes Brimborium einen guten Salat oder ein kaltes oder warmes Sandwich essen – alle 50 Variationen werden immer frisch zubereitet und tragen den Namen eines Freundes.

Cette sandwicherie sans prétention jouit d'un joli emplacement sur le pittoresque Passeig del Born. L'intérieur décontracté a été conçu par Cesc Pons, et une immense peinture murale du célèbre illustrateur Jordi Labanda donne à l'ensemble une note stylistique. Ici, on peut déguster en toute simplicité une délicieuse salade ou un sandwich chaud ou froid. Les cinquante variétés, toutes très fraîches, portent le nom d'un ami du propriétaire.

8 Café/Café/Café

Tèxtil Cafè
Carrer de Montcada 12
08003 Barcelona
Tel: +34 93 268 25 98
www.textilcafe.com
Tues/Wed 10am–8.30pm, Thurs/Sun 10am–midnight, Fri/Sat 10am–1am
Metro: L4 Jaume I

The tiny (5–6 table) Tèxtil Cafè is just across the way from the Picasso Museum (which has become very commercialized – now you can buy Picasso-themed coffee cups, erasers, silk scarves and even jigsaw puzzles). It is also a short step away from the crowded Carrer de Montcada, in the inner courtyard of the 13th-century Palau del

Marquès de Lló. This romantic oasis of peace and quiet is the ideal place to enjoy a "café con leche" far from the madding crowd.

Gegenüber dem inzwischen sehr touristischen Picasso-Museum (dort gibt es Picasso-Bilder auf Kaffeetassen, Radiergummis, Seidenschals und Puzzles zu kaufen) findet man das Tèxtil Cafè mit gerade einmal fünf oder sechs Tischen. Es liegt ein paar Schritte jenseits der überlaufenen Carrer de Montcada im Hof des Palau del Marquès de Lló, der aus dem 13. Jahrhundert stammt. In dieser romantischen Oase der Ruhe, umgeben von mittelalterlichem Gemäuer, kann man wunderbar einen „café con leche" trinken und den Rummel vergessen.

Juste en face du musée Picasso qui attire une foule de touristes (on peut y acheter des tasses, des gommes, des carrés en soie et des puzzles Picasso), se trouve le Tèxtil Cafè avec ses cinq ou six tables au maximum. Il est situé à quelques pas de la très fréquentée Carrer de Montcada dans la cour du Palau del Marquès de Lló, datant du XIIIe siècle. Dans cet oasis entouré de murailles moyenâgeuses, vous pourrez boire un « café con leche » en toute tranquillité.

9 Espadrilles/Espadrilles/Espadriles

La Manual Alpargatera
Carrer d'Avinyó 7
08002 Barcelona
Tel: +34 93 301 01 72
www.lamanual.net
Daily 9.30am–1.30pm and 4.30pm–8pm
Metro: L3 Liceu; L4 Jaume I

The first shoes, made from natural fibre and cotton or linen, made their fashion debut about 4,000 years ago. This famous shop is where you'll find the latest styles, in all imaginable colour combinations, for men, women and children. The "espardenyes" are still manufactured using traditional techniques, but are so durable nowadays that you can toss them in the washing machine.

Die ersten Schuhe aus Naturfasern und

9

10

Baumwolle oder Leinen trugen die Menschen schon vor rund 4000 Jahren – in diesem berühmten Laden findet man die Modelle der Moderne in allen nur erdenklichen Farbkombinationen und für Damen, Herren sowie Kinder. Hergestellt werden die „espardenyes" noch immer nach traditionellen Techniken, sie sind aber inzwischen so haltbar, dass man sie sogar in die Waschmaschine stecken kann.

Il y a 4000 ans, les hommes portaient déjà des espadrilles. Dans ce célèbre magasin, vous trouverez les modèles des temps modernes, pour hommes, femmes et enfants, et dans toutes les couleurs possibles et imaginables. Les « espardenyes » sont encore fabriquées selon des techniques traditionnelles, mais elles sont devenues si résistantes qu'on peut les laver à la machine.

10 Fresh fish/Frischer Fisch/Poisson frais

La Paradeta
Carrer Comercial 7
08003 Barcelona
Tel: +34 93 268 19 39
www.laparadeta.com
Tues–Fri 8am–11.30pm, Sat 1pm–4pm
and 8pm–midnight, Sun 1pm–4pm
Metro: L4 Barceloneta; Jaume I

As you enter, you choose the fish you'd like to eat – the fresh catch is laid out in a display case on ice. A short while later, your beautifully prepared seafood is handed back to you, over the counter. I recommend trying one of the many local wines on the list as an accompaniment. Always simple and fresh, always tasty.

Gleich am Eingang, wo der frische Fang auf Eis präsentiert wird, sucht man sich den Fisch aus, den man essen möchte. Wenig später wird das zubereitete Gericht auch schon über die Theke gereicht – dazu empfehle ich einen der lokalen Weine, die es hier in großer Auswahl gibt. Immer unkompliziert und immer lecker.

Dès l'entrée, vous choisirez parmi les poissons fraîchement pêchés disposés sur la glace, celui que vous désirez consommer. Peu de temps après, le plat sortira déjà des cuisines, prêt à la dégustation. Je vous conseille de boire en accompagnement un des petits vins locaux qui sont proposés ici en grand nombre. Des vins tout simples et toujours délicieux.

Personal discoveries/Eigene Entdeckungen/Découvertes personnelles :

Grand Hotel Central

Via Laietana, 30   08003 Barcelona
☎ +34 93 295 79 00   ☐ +34 93 268 12 15
info@grandhotelcentral.com
www.grandhotelcentral.com
Metro: L4 Jaume
Booking: www.great-escapes-hotels.com

Grand Hotel Central

The Grand Hotel Central is right in the thick of things on the busy Via Laietana, just around the corner from the Mercat de Santa Caterina. The market, with its wonderfully colourful corrugated roof, has quickly become a new landmark in the city since it opened in 2005. My tip: have your morning coffee with an "ensaimada" (a little pastry) in the market bar along with the housewives and street cleaners (who cheerfully order red wine even at this early hour!). Then, if you want to take things easy, you can go back to the hotel's roof terrace and relax by the Infinity Pool, with its spectacular view of Barcelona. If the view isn't stimulating enough, then read Federico García Lorca's "Blood Wedding" and have a "cerveza". The rooms have wooden floors, are intelligently laid out and are furnished with natural fabrics in shades of chocolate brown. Even the smallest rooms feel spacious. The only drawback is that the hotel doesn't have a cosy bar.

Das Grand Hotel Central liegt zentral – an der verkehrsreichen Via Laietana und um die Ecke vom Mercat de Santa Caterina. Dieser Markt wurde 2005 eingeweiht und mit seinem wunderbar gewellten bunten Dach in kurzer Zeit zu einem neuen Wahrzeichen der Stadt. Mein Tipp ist es, den Morgenkaffee mit einer „ensaimada" in der Marktbar einzunehmen (neben Hausfrauen und Straßenfegern, die schon um diese Uhrzeit gerne Rotwein bestellen). Danach kann man, wenn man gut Ding Weile sein lassen möchte, zurück auf die Dachterrasse des Hotels und am Infinity-Pool entspannen – von dort eröffnet sich ein spektakulärer Blick über Barcelona. Falls einem diese Aussicht noch nicht genügt, liest man „Bluthochzeit" von Federico García Lorca und trinkt eine „cerveza". Die Zimmer haben Holzböden, sind intelligent strukturiert und in Schokotönen mit Naturmaterialien eingerichtet; selbst die kleinsten Räume wirken noch großzügig. Leider besitzt das Hotel keine gemütliche Bar.

Le Grand Hotel Central est vraiment central puisqu'il est situé sur la très fréquentée Via Laietana et à l'angle du Mercat de Santa Caterina. Inauguré en 2005, ce marché est très vite devenu un nouveau symbole de la ville avec son magnifique toit ondulé. Je vais vous donner un tuyau : prenez votre premier café avec une « ensaimada » au bistrot du marché (à côté des ménagères et des balayeurs qui commandent volontiers un verre de rouge à cette heure). Après, vous pourrez retourner à l'hôtel et vous relaxer à la piscine Infinity, située sur le toit, et d'où vous aurez une vue spectaculaire sur Barcelone. Si la vue ne vous suffit pas, vous pourrez lire « Les Noces de sang » de Federico García Lorca tout en sirotant une « cerveza ». Les chambres ont des sols en bois, sont intelligemment structurées, sont aménagées avec des matériaux naturels et même les pièces les plus petites semblent spacieuses. Petit bémol, l'hôtel ne possède pas de bar.

Rates: Single and double rooms from 185 €, suites from 385 €. Breakfast 18 €.
Rooms: 147 rooms and suites.
Cuisine: Restaurant Actual serves Mediterranean and Catalan specialities.
History: Opened in November 2005.
X-Factor: The roof pool with a 360-degree view of Barcelona.
Internet: One hour for 6 €, 24 hours for 14 € (WLAN in the lobby, cable in the rooms).

Preise: EZ/DZ ab 185€, Suite ab 385 €. Frühstück 18 €.
Zimmer: 147 Zimmer und Suiten.
Küche: Im Restaurant Actual bekommt man mediterrane und katalanische Spezialitäten.
Geschichte: Im November 2005 eröffnet.
X-Faktor: Der Dachpool mit 360-Grad-Blick über Barcelona.
Internet: 1 Stunde 6 €, 24 Stunden 14 € (WLAN in der Lobby, Kabel im Zimmer).

Prix : Chambre simple ou double à partir de 185 €, suite à partir de 385 €. Petit-déjeuner 18 €.
Chambres : 147 chambres et suites.
Restauration : Spécialités méditerranéennes et catalanes au restaurant Actual.
Histoire : A ouvert ses portes en novembre 2005.
Le « petit plus » : La piscine sur le toit avec sa vue panoramique sur Barcelone.
Internet : 1 heure 6 €, 24 heures 14 € (WLAN dans le lobby, câble dans la chambre).

1

2

3

1   Church/Kirche/Église

Església de Sant Sever
Carrer de Sant Sever 9-11
08002 Barcelona
Tel: +34 93 318 16 81
Metro: L3 Liceu; L4 Jaume I

This richly decorated Baroque church, covered with gold, stands right beside Hotel Neri (see p. 66) – actually it doesn't stand as much as hide. When you walk through the narrow alley of Carrer de Sant Sever, you'll notice a simple entrance. If the hotel gate is open, you can peep through a glass door into the church – a well camouflaged gem.

Diese reich verzierte, über und über mit Gold bedeckte Barockkirche steht direkt neben dem Hotel Neri (siehe Seite 66) – beziehungsweise versteckt sich dort: Wenn man durch die enge Gasse Carrer de Sant Sever geht, kommt man an einen einfachen Eingang und kann – sofern das Holzportal geöffnet ist – durch eine Glastür in die Kirche spähen. Ein gut getarntes Juwel.

Richement décorée et couverte de dorures, cette église baroque se trouve juste à côté de l'hôtel Neri (voir page 66) et passe presque inaperçue. En marchant dans la ruelle Carrer de Sant Sever, on découvrira une entrée toute simple et l'on pourra, si le portail en bois est ouvert, jeter un coup d'œil dans l'église à travers la porte en verre. Un bijou bien dissimulé.

2   Café & tapas/Café & Tapas/
     Café & tapas

La Torna
Mercat de Santa Caterina
Avinguda de Francesc Cambó 16
08003 Barcelona
Tel: +34 93 319 58 21
Daily 8am–11pm
Metro: L4 Jaume I

Unspectacular, unpretentious, unknown and frequented almost exclusively by the local residents, La Torna is my favourite

bar for a "cortado" in the morning. There is no particular reason to love this bar, apart from the fact that it is located in the new and very atmospheric Santa Caterina market halls, the coffee tastes fantastic and the tapas are fresh and appetizing. Here you really can imagine you are living in Barcelona.

Unspektakulär, unprätentiös, unbekannt und fast nur von Einheimischen besucht, ist La Torna meine Lieblingsbar, um morgens einen „cortado" zu trinken. Es gibt keinen besonderen Grund, diese Bar zu mögen, aber sie liegt in den neuen und doch so atmosphärischen Markthallen von Santa Caterina, der Kaffee schmeckt herrlich, und die Tapas sind ganz frisch und lecker. Hier fühlt man sich, als ob man in Barcelona leben würde.

Éffacé, sans prétention, peu connu et pratiquement fréquenté que par les autochtones, La Torna est mon bar préféré pour boire un « cortado » le matin. Il n'existe aucune raison particulière pour aimer ce bar sauf qu'il se trouve dans les nouvelles halles de Santa Caterina, que le café y est délicieux et que les tapas sont frais et exquis. Ici on se sent comme si on vivait à Barcelone.

3   Coffee roasters/Kaffeerösterei/
     Torréfaction

Cafés El Magnífico
Carrer de l'Argenteria 64
08003 Barcelona
Tel: +34 93 310 33 61
www.cafeselmagnifico.com
Mon–Fri 9am–1.30pm and 4pm–8pm,
Sat 10am–2pm
Metro: L4 Jaume I

Freshly roasted coffee is one of the most delicious smells in the world. In this wonderful old (1919) coffee-roasting house the roasting machines are in the salesrooms, piled high with fat jute sacks filled with beans from all over the world. You can even have a little sampler. El Magnífico is run by Salvador Sans Velasco, who is considered the best coffee roaster in town, and is well known in Barcelona and beyond.

Frisch gerösteter Kaffee ist einer der köstlichsten Düfte überhaupt. In dieser wunderschönen alten Kaffeerösterei aus dem Jahr 1919 stehen die Röstmaschinen direkt im Verkaufsraum, wo sich auch die Jutesäcke mit den Bohnen aus aller Welt stapeln. Man kann sogar im Stehen eine kleine Kostprobe nehmen. El Magnífico wird von Salvador Sans Velasco geführt, der als bester Kaffeeröster der Stadt gilt und weit über ihre Grenzen hinaus bekannt ist.

Le café qui vient d'être torréfié a un arôme incomparable. Dans ce merveilleux établissement de torréfaction datant de 1919, tout se trouve dans une même salle : les machines, le comptoir et les sacs de jute qui contiennent les grains venant du monde entier. On peut même faire une petite dégustation. El Magnífico est géré par Salvador Sans Velasco, considéré comme le meilleur torréfacteur de la ville et dont la réputation dépasse de loin les frontières du pays.

4   Cookies/Kekse/Biscuits

Demasié
Carrer de la Princesa 28
08003 Barcelona
Tel: +34 93 310 42 95
www.demasie.es
Mon–Sat 10.30am–9pm, Sun midday–8pm
Metro: L4 Jaume I

The aroma that hits you when you enter this shop is to die for. And there is nothing to distract you from your pursuit of cookie nirvana: the minimalist interior and straightforward design of the packaging emphasizes the quality of these little baked treasures. Here, Catalan tradition is skilfully combined with design-crazy Barcelona. You can choose from simple butter biscuits, cookies with white chocolate, lemon or even hot chillies, or savoury delicacies flavoured with Parmesan, rosemary or truffles. I have no idea what "Demasié" means, but to my ears it sounds like "amnesia", which is what you feel the moment you smell those cookies …

Der Duft beim Betreten des Ladens ist betörend. Und nichts lenkt von diesem

4

5

Aroma ab – das minimalistische Interieur und schlichte Verpackungsdesign betonen die Qualität der kleinen gebackenen Köstlichkeiten. Ob einfache Butterkekse, Gebäck mit weißer Schokolade, Zitrone oder gar scharfen Chilis oder salzige Köstlichkeiten mit Parmesan-, Rosmarin- oder Trüffelgeschmack: Gekonnt verbinden sich hier katalanische Tradition und das designverrückte Barcelona. Ich weiß nicht, was „Demasié" bedeutet, aber für mich klingt es nach „Amnesie", wenn man die Kekse nur riecht …

Dès que l'on entre dans le magasin, un parfum enivrant vient vous chatouiller les narines. L'intérieur minimaliste et l'emballa-ge sobre ne détournent en rien l'attention, mettant seulement en valeur la qualité des délicieux biscuits : qu'il s'agisse de petit-beurre tout simples, de gâteaux au choco-lat blanc, au citron ou même au chili, ou encore de gâteaux salés au parmesan, au romarin ou aux truffes. Ici la tradition catalane se marie avec bonheur à la folie du design barcelonaise. J'ignore ce que signifie « Demasié », mais pour moi cela sonne comme « amnésie» quand je sens l'odeur de ces biscuits …

5   Fusion restaurant/Fusion-Restaurant/
     Fusion Restaurant

Salero
Carrer del Rec 60
08003 Barcelona
Tel: +34 93 319 80 22
Mon–Wed 1.30pm–4pm and 9pm–
midnight, Thurs/Fri 1pm–4pm and
9pm–1am, Sat 9pm–1am
Metro: L4 Barceloneta

Another restaurant designed by Pilar Líbano (Carmelitas, see p. 21), Salero radiates light and airiness. Housed in a former salt warehouse, the restaurant is decorated completely in white, right down to the white lilies on the tables. The furni-ture is a skilful combination of antique flea-market finds and industrially produced chairs and objects – it has a certain New York flair. So does the Japanese-inflected fusion cuisine, which attracts a young and modern clientele.

Ein weiteres Restaurant der Designerin Pilar Líbano (Carmelitas, siehe Seite 21), das Leichtigkeit und Luftigkeit ausstrahlt. In einem ehemaligen Salzlager unterge-bracht, ist das Dekor ganz in Weiß gehalten, bis hin zu den weißen Lilien auf den Tischen. Der Möbel-Mix aus antiken Flohmarktfun-den und industriell gefertigten Stühlen und Gegenständen ist gekonnt – er besitzt New Yorker Flair. Ebenso die Fusion-Küche mit japanischen Einflüssen, die ein junges, modernes Publikum anzieht.

Autre restaurant de la créatrice Pilar Líbano (Carmelitas, voir page 21), qui dégage une impression de légèreté. Situé dans un ancien entrepôt de sel, son décor est com-plètement blanc jusqu'aux lis sur les tables. Les meubles anciens provenant de marchés aux puces sont judicieusement combinés avec les chaises et les objets fabriqués en série. On se croirait à New York. Cela vaut également pour la « cuisine-fusion » avec ses influences japonaises, qui attire un public jeune et moderne.

Personal discoveries/Eigene
Entdeckungen/Découvertes personnelles :

El Born

1 Modern tapas bar/Moderne Tapas-Bar/Bar à tapas moderne
Santa Maria

2 Kitchenware/Küchenwaren/Ustensiles de cuisine
Targa

3 Catalan restaurant/Katalanisches Restaurant/
Restaurant catalan
Restaurant Borràs l'Econòmic

4 Imported speciality foods/Kaufmannsladen/Épicerie
E & A Gispert

5 Museum & café/Museum & Café/Musée & café
MFM Museu Frederic Marès
(Map on page 64/65)

6 Pastry shop/Konditorei/Pâtisserie
Brunells

---

1 Church & architecture/Kirche & Architektur/
Église & architecture
Santa Maria del Mar

2 Fish restaurant/Fischrestaurant/Restaurant de poissons
Passadís del Pep

3 Concept store/Concept-Store/Concept Store
Lobby

4 Tapas & cava/Tapas & Cava/Tapas & Cava
El Xampanyet

5 Bicycle hire/Fahrradverleih/Location de vélos
Un Cotxe Menys
Bicicleta Barcelona

6 Tapas bar/Tapas-Bar/Bar à tapas
Mundial Bar

Hotel
Banys Orientals

Carrer de l'Argenteria, 37   08003 Barcelona
☎ +34 93 268 84 60   📠 +34 93 268 84 61
reservas@hotelbanysorientals.com
www.hotelbanysorientals.com
Metro: L4 Jaume I
Booking: www.great-escapes-hotels.com

Hotel Banys Orientals

What makes this one of the most popular hotels in Barcelona? It could be the elegant interior by Lázaro Rosa Violán, who also designed the Hotel Pulitzer (see p. 52). Or maybe it's the fantastic location in the centre of El Born, with its picturesque alleyways, shops, bars, restaurants and sights. Finally, there's the price, which starts at less than 100 € a night. In 2004, the renowned travel magazine Condé Nast Traveller put Hotel Banys Orientals on its list of ten best Mediterranean hotels. Tastefully decorated rooms with dark floor boards, light wooden furniture, airy white curtains, light grey walls and designer four-poster beds await the visitor behind the historic Spanish façade. Antique and modern elements are beautifully combined: light, transparent chairs by Philippe Starck stand beside heavy Louis XV-style armchairs, old engravings adorn the walls, while the bathrooms are ultra-modern. The new suites in the adjoining building are also very nicely done.

Die eleganten Interieurs von Lázaro Rosa Violán, die auch das Hotel Pulitzer gestaltet hat (siehe Seite 52), die fantastische Lage mitten im Born mit seinen malerischen Gassen, Läden, Bars, Restaurants und Sehenswürdigkeiten sowie der Preis – ab knapp 100 € pro Nacht – machen dieses Hotel zu einer der beliebtesten Unterkünfte in Barcelona. 2004 wurde es vom renommierten Reisemagazin Condé Nast Traveller sogar auf die Liste der 10 besten Hotels im Mittelmeerraum gesetzt. Hinter der historischen spanischen Fassade warten geschmackvoll eingerichtete Zimmer mit dunklen Dielenböden, hellen Holzmöbeln, duftig-weißen Vorhängen, hellgrauen Wänden und Designerhimmelbetten. Antike und moderne Accessoires werden toll gemischt – wie durchsichtige, leichte Stühle von Philippe Starck und schwere Sessel im Louis-XV-Stil, alte Stiche an der Wand und modernste Badezimmer. Sehr gelungen sind auch die neuen Suiten im Nebengebäude.

Les intérieurs élégants de Lázaro Rosa Violán, qui a aussi décoré l'hôtel Pulitzer (voir page 52), l'emplacement fantastique en plein cœur du quartier El Born avec ses ruelles pittoresques, ses boutiques, ses bistrots, ses restaurants et ses curiosités, ainsi que les premiers prix des chambres en dessous de 100 € font de cet hôtel l'un des hébergements les plus populaires de Barcelone. En 2004, le célèbre magazine de voyage Condé Nast Traveller l'a même inscrit sur sa liste des dix meilleurs hôtels du bassin méditerranéen. Derrière sa façade historique vous attendent des chambres aménagées avec goût : planchers sombres, meubles en bois clair, rideaux blancs et vaporeux, murs gris clair et lits design à baldaquin. L'ancien et le moderne s'y combinent à merveille : chaises légères et transparentes de Philippe Starck, lourds fauteuils Louis XV, gravures anciennes et salles de bains ultra-modernes. Les nouvelles suites dans l'annexe sont également très réussies.

Rates: Single rooms from 82 €, double rooms from 98 €, suites from 129 €. Breakfast 10 €.
Rooms: 43 rooms in the main building, 13 suites in the adjoining building.
Cuisine: The stylish restaurant offers traditional Catalan dishes, prepared with a contemporary flair.
History: The hotel opened in 2002; the classy suites have been available since 2005.
X-Factor: Excellent value for money.
Internet: Free of charge (high-speed).

Preise: EZ ab 82 €, DZ ab 98 €, Suite ab 129 €. Frühstück 10 €.
Zimmer: 43 Zimmer im Haupthaus, 13 Suiten im Nebengebäude.
Küche: Im stilvollen Restaurant steht traditionelle katalanische Küche auf der Karte, die modern interpretiert wird.
Geschichte: Das Hotel wurde in 2002 eröffnet, die schicken Suiten bestehen seit 2005.
X-Faktor: Das hervorragende Preis-Leistungs-Verhältnis.
Internet: Kostenfrei (highspeed).

Prix : Chambre simple à partir de 82 €, double à partir de 98 €, suite à partir de 129 €. Petit déjeuner 10 €.
Chambres : 43 chambres dans le bâtiment principal, 13 suites dans l'annexe.
Restauration : Le restaurant distingué sert une cuisine catalane traditionnelle réinterprétée de façon moderne.
Histoire : L'hôtel a ouvert en 2002, les suites élégantes existent depuis 2005.
Le « petit plus » : Excellent rapport qualité/prix.
Internet : Gratuit (haut débit).

1

2

3

1 Modern tapas bar/Moderne Tapas-
Bar/Bar à tapas moderne

Santa Maria
Carrer del Comerç 17
08003 Barcelona
Tel: +34 93 315 12 27
www.santamaria.biz
Tues–Sat 1.30pm–3.30pm and
8.30pm–midnight
Metro: L4 Jaume I; L1 Arc de Triomf

Ferran Adrià, a Catalan, revolutionised
the international restaurant world with his
culinary wizardry. Some of his students
have now opened up their own restaurants
and tapas bars in Barcelona, places where
the waiting list is not as lengthy, nor the
prices as upmarket as in the world-famous elBulli. Santa Maria (named after
Columbus's first ship) is the most charming
of these new venues. Head chef Paco
Guzmán serves avant-garde creations like
lettuce with ice cream, and duck with bean
purée. His tapas are very popular with the
creative types – gallery owners and multi-
media artists – in the neighbourhood.

Der Katalane Ferran Adrià hat mit seiner
neuen, alchemistischen Küche die internationale Restaurantwelt revolutioniert.
Einige seiner Schüler haben inzwischen
Lokale und Tapas-Bars in Barcelona
eröffnet – hier sind die Wartezeiten noch
nicht so lang und die Preise noch nicht so
gehoben wie im weltberühmten elBulli.
Santa Maria (nach Kolumbus' erstem Schiff
benannt) ist die charmanteste dieser neuen
Locations; Chefkoch Paco Guzmán kreiert
Avantgardistisches wie Salat mit Eiscreme
oder Ente mit Bohnenmus. Seine Tapas
sind bei den Kreativen, Galeristen und
Multimediakünstlern des Viertels beliebt.

Le Catalan Ferran Adrià a révolutionné la
gastronomie internationale avec sa nouvelle
cuisine alchimique. Depuis, quelques-uns
de ses élèves ont ouvert des établissements et des bars à tapas à Barcelone.
Ici, les prix ne sont pas encore aussi salés
qu'au célèbre elBulli et il n'est pas nécessaire de réserver autant à l'avance. Santa
Maria (nommé d'après la caravelle de
Christophe Colom) est le plus charmant de
ces nouveaux lieux. Le chef Paco Guzmán
crée des plats avant-gardistes comme la
salade à la crème glacée ou le canard à la
mousse de haricots. Ses tapas sont très
prisés des créateurs, des galeristes et des
artistes multimédias du quartier.

2 Kitchenware/Küchenwaren/
Ustensiles de cuisine

Targa
Pla de Palau 5-6
08003 Barcelona
Tel: +34 93 319 92 41
Mon–Fri 9am–1.30pm and 4pm–8pm,
Sat 9am–midday
Metro: L4 Barceloneta

The new designer kitchen tools may be
eye-candy, but they are still no competition
for classic Mediterranean kitchen utensils.
Here you'll find everything: stainless-steel
espresso machines, olive oil decanters
that don't drip, gorgeous enamel dishes
in brilliant red and, of course, every size
of paella frying pan under the sun. All
will make lovely souvenirs of your Spanish
holiday. Targa offers the best selection
in the city, and even just browsing the
window display is a pleasure. (Every item
is arranged according to shape and size.)

Klassische Küchenutensilien aus dem
Mittelmeerraum schlagen bis heute jede
noch so hübsche Designerware. Espresso-
maschinen aus Edelstahl, Olivenölkännchen,
die nicht tropfen, bildschönes Emaillege-
schirr in leuchtendem Rot und natürlich
Paellapfannen in allen Größen sind immer
wieder ein schönes Mitbringsel aus dem
Spanienurlaub. Targa hat die beste Auswahl;
und bereits der Blick ins Schaufenster ist
hier ein Genuss.

Les ustensiles de cuisine classiques éclip-
sent aujourd'hui encore les plus jolis objets
design. Percolateurs en acier inox, huiliers
qui ne gouttent pas, vaisselle en émail
rouge vif et, bien sûr, poêles à paella de
toutes tailles sont des cadeaux qui font
toujours plaisir. Targa a le meilleur choix ;
et on ne se lasse pas d'admirer sa vitrine :
tous les objets y sont rangés suivant leur
taille et leur forme.

3 Catalan restaurant/Katalanisches
Restaurant/Restaurant catalan

Restaurant Borràs l'Econòmic
Plaça de Sant Agustí Vell 13
08003 Barcelona
Tel: +34 93 319 64 94
Daily 1pm–4pm
Metro: L1 Arc de Triomf

True to its name, the restaurant serves
very inexpensive, homemade Catalan
meals in an atmosphere that's remained
unchanged since 1932. The handwritten
menu changes daily, and has some delicious
dishes, always freshly prepared – a perfect
stop for a good lunch. The interior is a lively
mixture of colourful Spanish tiles and lots
of old pictures and mirrors. On warm days,
you can sit outside in the romantic Plaça
de Sant Agustí Vell.

Nomen est omen: In dem seit 1932 unver-
änderten Ambiente gibt es sehr preiswerte,
hausgemachte katalanische Menüs. Die
Speisekarte wechselt täglich, ist hand-
geschrieben und umfasst immer frisch
zubereitete Köstlichkeiten – wunderbar
für ein gutes Mittagessen. Das Interieur ist
eine wilde Mischung aus bunten spanischen
Fliesen, vielen alten Bildern und Spiegeln;
an warmen Tagen kann man auf der romantischen Plaça de Sant Agustí Vell sitzen.

Nomen est omen : dans une ambiance
restée la même depuis 1932, on vous sert
des menus catalans pas chers et faits
maison. Écrite à la main, la carte change
tous les jours et propose toujours des
mets frais et délicieux. Parfait pour un
bon déjeuner. L'intérieur mélange
allégrement les carreaux espagnols de
couleur et beaucoup d'anciens tableaux
et miroirs. Les jours de chaleur, on peut
s'asseoir dehors sur la romantique Plaça
de Sant Agustí Vell.

4 Imported speciality foods/
Kaufmannsladen/Épicerie

E & A Gispert
Carrer dels Sombrerers 23
08003 Barcelona

4

5

6

Tel: +34 93 319 75 35
www.casagispert.com
Tues–Fri 9.30am–2pm and 4pm–7.30pm,
Sat 10am–2pm and 5pm–8pm
Metro: L4 Jaume I

This imported speciality food store has been selling dried fruit and roasted nuts for more than 150 years. The shop is titillating to the senses, and probably the only place left in Europe where a Roman-style drying and roasting oven is still in use – the resulting fragrance is irresistible. The shop front with its wooden ornamentation, wooden barrels and sacks of nuts and coffee alongside attractively wrapped culinary delights is very picturesque.

Seit mehr als 150 Jahren gibt es in diesem Kolonialwarenladen getrocknete Früchte und geröstete Nüsse. Das Geschäft ist ein Gedicht der Sinne und wahrscheinlich der einzige Ort in Europa, an dem noch ein Röst- und Dörrofen römischer Art benutzt wird – der Duft ist dementsprechend verführerisch. Die Ladenfront mit Holzverzierung, die Holzfässer und Säcke voller Nüsse und Kaffee sowie die schön verpackten Köstlichkeiten geben einfach ein malerisches Bild ab.

Cette épicerie vend des fruits secs et des noisettes grillées depuis plus d'un siècle et demi. Le magasin est probablement le seul lieu en Europe où l'on utilise encore un grilloir et un séchoir romains. Le parfum qui s'en dégage est tout simplement irrésistible. Les boiseries du magasin, les tonneaux en bois et les sacs pleins de noisettes et de café ainsi que les friandises joliment emballées offrent un tableau des plus pittoresques.

5   Museum & café/Museum & Café/
    Musée & café

MFM Museu Frederic Marès
Plaça de Sant Iu 5-6
08002 Barcelona
Tel: +34 93 256 35 00 (museum)
Tel: +34 93 268 25 98 (café)
www.museumares.bcn.es
www.textilcafe.com
Tues–Sat 10am–7pm, Sun 10am–3pm.

Metro: L4 Jaume I
(Map on page 64/65)

This museum houses the eclectic collection of the sculptor Frederic Marès, who lives in part of the old palace. Even more charming is the little café tucked away in the courtyard (at the entrance to the museum), open from April to September. Hidden away from the tourist trail, on a little street behind the cathedral, you can enjoy the romantic atmosphere, listen to the babbling fountain and gaze into the trees heavy with oranges – an ideal coffee-break stop.

Das Museum beherbergt die eklektische Kunstsammlung des Bildhauers Frederic Marès, der in einem Teil des alten Palastes wohnte. Doch noch schöner ist das kleine Café im Hof (am Eingang des Museums), das von April bis September geöffnet hat. Es versteckt sich abseits der Touristenpfade in einer kleinen Straße hinter der Kathedrale. Hier genießt man die romantische Atmosphäre, hört dem Springbrunnen beim Plätschern zu und blickt in Bäume, die mit Orangen überladen sind – ideal für einen entspannenden Kaffee.

Le musée abrite la collection éclectique d'œuvres d'art du sculpteur Frederic Marès, qui a résidé dans une partie du vieux palais. Mais le petit café dans la cour (à l'entrée du musée), qui est ouvert d'avril à septembre, vaut encore plus le déplacement. Loin des circuits touristiques, il est niché dans une petite rue derrière la cathédrale. Avec son atmosphère romantique, le clapotis de sa fontaine et ses arbres couverts d'oranges, il est l'endroit idéal pour boire un café en toute tranquillité.

6   Pastry shop/Konditorei/Pâtisserie

Brunells
Carrer de la Princesa 22
08003 Barcelona
Tel: +34 93 319 68 25
Mon–Sat 8:30am–8pm
Metro: L4 Jaume I

This old pastry shop opened in 1889 and very little has changed since, either in the shop decoration or the range of cakes and cookies, which are still baked over a wood fire. Try the irresistible house speciality: Roques de Montserrat. This meringue-like little cake was named after the Montserrat mountain because of its shape, and it just melts on your tongue. In addition, Brunells sells all sorts of Turrones (honey and almond confectionery), biscuits and delicious fruit that's filled with ice cream.

1889 wurde diese alte Konditorei eröffnet, und seitdem hat sich nur wenig verändert – weder die Ladeneinrichtung noch das Angebot an Süßigkeiten. Diese werden auch immer noch auf Holzfeuer gebacken, darunter die verlockende Spezialität des Hauses, die „Roques de Montserrat": Das baiserähnliche Gebäck wurde wegen seiner Form nach dem Berg Montserrat außerhalb Barcelonas benannt und schmilzt zart auf der Zunge. Außerdem bietet Brunells alle Arten an „turrones" (Honig-Mandel-Konfekt), Kekse, Kuchen und köstliche, mit Eis gefüllte Früchte.

Ouverte en 1889, cette ancienne pâtisserie-confiserie n'a guère changé depuis, qu'il s'agisse de sa décoration intérieure ou de ses gâteaux. La cuisson de ces derniers se fait encore au feu de bois, comme pour celle de la spécialité de la maison, la succulente « Roques de Montserrat ». Nommé à cause de sa forme d'après la montagne de Montserrat, ce gâteau meringué fond délicieusement dans la bouche. Brunells propose aussi toutes sortes de tourons (confiseries au miel et aux amandes), de biscuits et de fruits givrés.

Personal discoveries/Eigene
Entdeckungen/Découvertes personnelles :

_____

_____

_____

_____

_____

Hotel
Chic & Basic

Carrer de la Princesa, 50   08003 Barcelona
☎ +34 93 295 46 52
born@chicandbasic.com
www.chicandbasic.com
Metro: L4 Jaume I; L1 Arc de Triomf
Booking: www.great-escapes-hotels.com

Hotel Chic & Basic

The Chic & Basic is an inexpensive but pretty hotel in the centre of El Born. It certainly is "chic", but is it "basic"? That adjective might refer to the price, or perhaps to the fact that there are only three room categories: XL, L and M. Xavier Claramunt skilfully transformed the elegant old building with its 5.5-metre-high staircase into a designer hotel in 2006. He retained the original plaster moulding on the ceilings, the marble and stone floors as well as the transom windows and doors, and combined these details with very modern technology and customised furniture. Everything is white on white, and the rooms can be bathed in changing colours by the use of an LED light system (an "innovation" that I could do without). A curtain of floor-length transparent plastic strings hangs in front of each door, and this effectively turns the corridors into sculpture gardens. There is also a very stylish but cosy lounge with huge sofas.

Das Chic & Basic ist ein preiswertes und gleichzeitig schönes Hotel mitten im Born. Ich finde es chic, aber nicht basic – doch vielleicht bezieht sich die Bezeichnung auf den Preis oder darauf, das es nur drei Zimmerkategorien gibt: XL, L und M. Der elegante Altbau mit einem 5,5 Meter hohen Marmortreppenhaus wurde von Xavier Claramunt gekonnt in ein Designhotel verwandelt. Dabei blieben die alten Stuckdecken, Marmor- und Steinböden, Sprossenfenster und -türen erhalten – aber mit sehr moderner Technik und eigens entworfenen Möbeln kombiniert. Alles ist Weiß in Weiß gehalten; durch ein LED-Lichtsystem können die Räume in wechselnde Farben getaucht werden (darauf könnte ich allerdings verzichten). Vor jeder Zimmertür hängt ein bodenlanger Vorhang aus durchsichtigen Plastikschnüren, was die Flure in einen Skulpturengarten verwandelt. Außerdem gibt es einen sehr stylischen und trotzdem gemütlichen Aufenthaltsraum mit überdimensionalen Sofas.

Situé en plein cœur du quartier El Born, le Chic & Basic est un hôtel à la fois beau et pas cher. Je le trouve chic, mais certainement pas basic – ce terme est peut-être une référence à son prix ou au fait qu'il n'y a que trois catégories de chambres : XL, L et M. Avec son escalier en marbre de 5,5 m de haut, cet immeuble ancien a été transformé avec talent en hôtel design par Xavier Claramunt. Ce dernier a conservé les plafonds en stuc, les sols de marbre et de pierre, ainsi que les portes et les fenêtres à croisillons tout en les combinant avec une technique sophistiquée et des meubles qu'il a dessinés lui-même. Les chambres sont toutes blanches et un système d'éclairage LED les plonge dans différentes couleurs (ce qui n'est pas nécessaire selon moi). Devant les portes des chambres sont accrochés des rideaux transparents de bandelettes en plastique qui métamorphosent le couloir en jardin de sculptures. Par ailleurs, il y a dans l'hôtel un salon très stylisé mais malgré tout confortable avec des canapés surdimensionnés.

Rates: Single and double rooms 95 €– 150 €. Breakfast 8 €.
Rooms: 31 rooms.
Cuisine: The White Bar next door serves breakfast and Catalan meals for lunch and dinner.
History: The hotel, which opened in 2006, is housed in a building dating from 1888, the year the World's Fair was held in Barcelona.
X-Factor: The hotel's own DJ plays music on Friday and Saturday evenings.
Internet: Free of charge in the "be yourself area", 9 € for 24 hours in your room (via LCD-TV).

Preise: EZ/DZ 95–150 €. Frühstück 8 €.
Zimmer: 31 Zimmer.
Küche: In der White Bar nebenan gibt es Frühstück sowie mittags und abends katalanische Menüs.
Geschichte: Das Hotel wurde 2006 eröffnet. Es ist in einem Altbau anno 1888 untergebracht – dem Jahr der Weltausstellung in Barcelona.
X-Faktor: Am Freitag- und Samstagabend legt der hoteleigene DJ auf.
Internet: Kostenfrei in der „be yourself area", im Zimmer 9 € für 24 Stunden (via LCD-TV).

Prix : Chambre simple ou double 95–150 €. Petit déjeuner 8 €.
Chambres : 31 chambres.
Restauration : Petit déjeuner et menus catalans midi et soir au White Bar situé à côté.
Histoire : Ouvert en 2006, l'hôtel se trouve dans un immeuble ancien datant de 1888, l'année de l'Exposition internationale à Barcelone.
Le « petit plus » : Musique avec DJ de l'hôtel le vendredi et le samedi soir.
Internet : Gratuit dans la « be yourself area », dans les chambres 9 € pour 24 heures (via LCD-TV).

Chic&basic is different. It's
concept. It's simple, it's s
surprising. It's open-minded, it's
It's fresh ideas. It's naughty
possible? Yes, it is. It's contemp
It's comfortable. It's a nightlife
It's easy to check in, it's easy
out. It's just easy. It's fusion, it's cos
culture. It's Spanish, it's English, it's
French, it's bla, bla, bla, it's li
Oh... It's Basic, that's what

1

2

3

1 Church & architecture/Kirche &
Architektur/Église & architecture

Santa Maria del Mar
Plaça de Santa Maria 1
08003 Barcelona
Tel: +34 93 310 23 90
Mon–Sat 9am–1.30pm and 4.30pm–8pm,
Sun 10am–1.30pm and 4.30pm–8pm
Metro: L4 Barceloneta

Le Corbusier called Santa Maria del Mar
the most beautiful church in Barcelona – it
is the other "must-see" Barcelona church
besides the Sagrada Família. Thanks to
its relatively short building period, from
1329 to 1383 (by contrast, Cologne
Cathedral took more than 600 years to
complete), it displays an unusually uniform
architectural style. From outside, it appears
rather sturdy, but inside, its Gothic proportions and the remarkable height of the
nave display a solemn elegance.

Le Corbusier bezeichnete Santa Maria del
Mar als die schönste Kirche Barcelonas
– und man sollte sie neben der Sagrada
Família wirklich einmal besuchen. Ihrer
kurzen Bauzeit von 1329 bis 1383 (für
den Kölner Dom brauchte man mehr als
600 Jahre) verdankt sie einen außergewöhnlich einheitlichen Stil. Von außen
betrachtet wirkt sie eher robust, innen aber
ist sie mit ihren gotischen Proportionen und
der beachtlichen Höhe des Mittelschiffs
von feierlicher Eleganz.

Considérée par Le Corbusier comme la plus
belle église de Barcelone, Santa Maria del
Mar doit faire partie du programme avec la
Sagrada Família. Elle doit son style éton-
namment homogène à sa courte durée de
construction de 1329 à 1383 (il fallut plus
de six siècles pour terminer la cathédrale
de Cologne). Plutôt trapue de l'extérieur,
elle dégage à l'intérieur une élégance so-
lennelle avec ses proportions gothiques et
la hauteur considérable de sa nef.

2 Fish restaurant/Fischrestaurant/
Restaurant de poissons

Passadís del Pep
Pla de Palau 2
08003 Barcelona
Tel: +34 93 310 10 21
www.passadis.com
Mon 9pm–11.30pm, Tues–Sat 1.30pm–
3.30pm and 9pm–11.30pm
Metro: L4 Barceloneta

You can be sure of one thing: this is probably the best fish restaurant in Barcelona.
What is not so sure is: will you be able to
find it? It's located at the end of a long,
dark corridor, and there aren't any sign-
posts. There's no English-language menu –
in fact, there's no menu at all. Guests just
accept the recommendations of the waiter
or chef. The proprietor, Pep Manubens,
also owns a more inexpensive and just as
popular alternative: the Cal Pep (Plaça
de les Olles 8, Tel: +34 93 310 76 91),
a legendary Mecca for tapas aficionados.

Sicher ist, dass dies eines der besten
Fischrestaurants von Barcelona ist; un-
sicher, ob man es auch findet. Fast ohne
Hinweisschild liegt es unspektakulär am
Ende eines langen, dunklen Korridors.
Gäste bekommen keine Speisekarte
(schon gar nicht auf Englisch), sondern
folgen einfach den Empfehlungen des
Obers oder Küchenchefs. Der Inhaber
Pep Manubens besitzt noch eine preis-
günstigere, aber ebenso beliebte Variante:
das Cal Pep (Plaça de les Olles 8,
Tel: +34 93 310 76 91), ein legendäres
Mekka für Tapas-Aficionados.

Une chose est sûre, ce restaurant de
poissons est l'un des meilleurs de
Barcelone. Ce qui est moins sûr en revan-
che, c'est de savoir si on le trouvera, vu sa
situation au bout d'un long corridor sombre. Les clients ne reçoivent pas de menu
mais suivent simplement les recommanda-
tions du serveur ou du chef. Pep Manubens
est également le propriétaire d'un autre
restaurant encore meilleur marché, mais
tout aussi prisé : le Cal Pep (Plaça de
les Olles 8, tél : +34 93 310 76 91), le
rendez-vous des aficionados des tapas.

3 Concept store/Concept-Store/
Concept Store

Lobby
Carrer de la Ribera 5
08003 Barcelona
Tel: +34 93 319 38 55
www.lobby-bcn.com
Mon–Sat 11am–9pm
Metro: L4 Barceloneta/Jaume I

Lobby is Barcelona's answer to the ultra-
trendy concept store Colette in Paris.
Smaller and less busy, the shop sells
unusual fashions by Spanish and international designers like Crea, Pleats Please by
Issey Miyake and Y-3. Cosmetic products
by Costiera, Laura Tonatto or Campos de
Ibiza are also on offer, as are books and
accessories.

Lobby ist die Antwort Barcelonas auf den
ultra-trendigen Concept-Store Colette in
Paris. Kleiner und ruhiger, wird hier außer-
gewöhnliche Mode von spanischen und
internationalen Designern wie Crea, Pleats
Please by Issey Miyake oder Y-3 verkauft.
Außerdem bekommt man Kosmetikpro-
dukte von Costiera, Laura Tonatto oder
Campos de Ibiza, Bücher und Accessoires.

Lobby est la réponse de Barcelone au
Concept Store Colette ultra tendance de
Paris. Plus petit et plus calme, il propose
des créations originales de designers
internationaux comme Crea, Pleats Please
by Issey Miyake ou Y-3. On peut en
outre y acheter des produits de beauté
de Costiera, Laura Tonatto ou Campos de
Ibiza, des livres et des accessoires.

4 Tapas & cava/Tapas & Cava/
Tapas & Cava

El Xampanyet
Carrer de Montcada 22
08003 Barcelona
Tel: +34 93 319 70 03
Tues–Sat midday–4pm and 7pm–11.30pm
Metro: L4 Jaume I

True to name: delicious, well-chilled champagne from Spain (cava) can be bought

4

5

6

here, at prices far lower than champagne with a French label. Freshly prepared little culinary delights are served along with the "cava". Although this cosy traditional bar is situated on the touristy Carrer de Montcada, it is still popular with the local residents and is always bustling – and we know why.

Wieder passt der Spruch nomen est omen: Hier erhält man köstlichen, gut gekühlten Champagner aus Spanien („cava"), der sehr viel preiswerter ist als die Sorte mit französischem Namen. Dazu gibt es frisch zubereitete kleine Leckereien. Die urige Bar liegt zwar auf der von Touristen frequentierten Carrer de Montcada, wird aber von den Einheimischen gern besucht und ist immer proppenvoll – das hat seinen Grund.

La formule nomen est omen s'applique ici aussi : on y trouve un délicieux champagne espagnol (« cava »), bien moins cher que son cousin français. Pour l'accompagner, vous pourrez vous régaler avec des amuse-gueule venant d'être préparés. Ce bar rustique se trouve certes sur la touristique carrer de Montcada, mais il est volontiers fréquenté par les autochtones et est toujours plein. Ce n'est pas sans raison.

5   Bicycle hire/Fahrradverleih/
     Location de vélos

Un Cotxe Menys
Bicicleta Barcelona
Carrer d'Esparteria 3
08003 Barcelona
Tel: +34 93 268 21 05
www.bicicletabarcelona.com
Mon–Sat 10am–7pm, Sun 10am–2pm
Prices: 5 € an hour, 15 € a day.
Metro: L4 Barceloneta/Jaume I

When you want to get away from the bustle of the city, or if you simply can't walk another step, then hire a bike and ride off towards the beach. You can pedal along by the sea for hours, enjoying the fantastic landscape and the clean, fresh air. Even Barcelona can be explored very nicely on a two-wheeler.

Wer dem Trubel in der Stadt entfliehen möchte oder einfach nicht mehr auf zwei

Beinen laufen kann, sollte sich ein Fahrrad leihen und Richtung Strand fahren. Von dort kann man stundenlang am Meer entlangrollen und die wunderschöne Aussicht sowie die gute Luft genießen. Und auch Barcelona selbst lässt sich wunderbar auf dem Stahlross erkunden.

Si vous voulez fuir l'agitation de la ville ou si vous en avez assez de marcher, allez donc louer un vélo pour faire un tour à la plage. Vous pourrez longer la côte pendant des heures tout en jouissant d'une vue saisissante et de la pureté de l'air. Mais la ville de Barcelone se visite aussi facilement à vélo.

6   Tapas bar/Tapas-Bar/Bar à tapas

Mundial Bar
Plaça de Sant Agustí Vell 1
08003 Barcelona
Tel: +34 93 319 90 56
Tues–Sun midday–4pm and 8pm–midnight,
Sun midday–4.30pm
Metro: L1 Arc de Triomf

This tapas bar on the pleasant Plaça de Sant Agustí Vell opened in 1925 and has been a neighbourhood favourite ever since. It is simple, unsophisticated and has a great atmosphere. You can drink beer, eat classic tapas (the grilled calamari, cooked mussels and ham are delicious) and you can even smoke (an activity forbidden in restaurants and pubs elsewhere in Spain).

An der intimen Plaça de Sant Agustí Vell gelegen, wurde diese Bar im Look der 1920er-Jahre 1925 eröffnet und erfreut sich seitdem regen Besuchs durch die Nachbarschaft. Sie ist schlicht, schnörkellos und voller Atmosphäre – hier kann man ein Bier trinken, einfache Tapas essen (lecker sind gegrillter Tintenfisch, gekochte Muscheln und Schinken) und sogar rauchen, was sonst in ganz Spanien in Restaurants sowie Kneipen nicht mehr erlaubt ist.

Situé sur une petite place intime, la plaça de Sant Agustí Vell, ce bar au look des années 20 a ouvert en 1925 et est, depuis, très couru des habitants du quartier. Il est simple, sans chichis et plein

d'ambiance. Ici, on peut siroter une bière, manger des tapas classiques (le calamar grillé, les moules et le jambon sont un délice) et même fumer, ce qui n'est plus permis dans les restaurants et bars dans toute l'Espagne.

Personal discoveries/Eigene
Entdeckungen/Découvertes personnelles :

_____

_____

_____

_____

_____

_____

_____

_____

_____

_____

_____

_____

_____

_____

_____

_____

_____

_____

La Barceloneta

Hotel Arts
Barcelona

Carrer de la Marina, 19-21   08005 Barcelona
☎ +34 93 221 10 00   ☐ +34 93 221 10 70
rc.bcnrz.reservations@ritzcarlton.com
www.ritzcarlton.com
Metro: L4 Ciutadella, Vila Olímpica
Booking: www.great-escapes-hotels.com

Hotel Arts Barcelona

Built in 1922 as the showcase hotel for the Olympics, and only recently modernised, the 44-storey Ritz Carlton is still the most elegant and luxurious modern hotel in Barcelona. Located right on the coast, it has magnificent views of Port Olímpic and Frank Gehry's huge flying fish sculpture. As you take in the amazing view of the pool framed by palm trees, or visit the excellent Six Senses Spa, and the gourmet restaurants, it will suddenly dawn on you that you really are on vacation, and the city is a backdrop for that holiday getaway. My preferred supper venue here is the Arola. The hotel rooms are decorated in beige, sand and ecru, a sharp contrast to the dark wood of the furniture. I recommend the corner junior suites on the top floors. From here, you get a stunning view of the Mediterranean and the city – you can see the Sagrada Família, as well as the latest addition to Barcelona's skyline, the striking Torre Agbar by Jean Nouvel.

Als Vorzeigehotel zu den Olympischen Spielen 1992 gebaut und erst vor Kurzem renoviert, ist dieses 44-geschossige Ritz-Carlton-Hotel bis heute das eleganteste moderne Hotel in Barcelona. Direkt am Meer gelegen, eröffnet es einen herrlichen Blick über den Port Olímpic und auf die riesige fliegende Fischskulptur von Frank Gehry – hier verspürt man Urlaubsfeeling, obwohl man sich in einer Großstadt befindet. Zu diesem Gefühl tragen auch der von Palmen umrahmte Pool, das herausragende Six Senses Spa sowie die Gourmetrestaurants bei, von denen mir das Arola am besten zum Dinieren gefällt. Die Zimmer sind in Beige, Sand und Ecru gehalten, kontrastiert vom dunklen Holz der Möbel. Ich empfehle eine der Junior Suiten in den Ecken der oberen Stockwerke. Diese Räume bieten eine atemberaubende Aussicht über das Mittelmeer und die Stadt – bis zur Sagrada Família sowie zum markanten Torre Agbar von Jean Nouvel, dem neuen Wahrzeichen in Barcelonas Skyline.

Construit à l'occasion des Jeux olympiques de 1992 et rénové depuis peu, ce Ritz-Carlton Hotel de quarante-quatre étages est à ce jour l'hôtel moderne le plus élégant de Barcelone. Situé en bord de mer, il offre une vue splendide sur le Port Olímpic et sur le poisson en acier de Frank Gehry – on se croirait en vacances alors que l'on se trouve dans une grande ville, impression que renforcent la piscine entourée de palmiers, le Six Senses Spa remarquable et les restaurants gastronomiques – l' « Arola » est mon préféré pour le dîner. Dans les chambres, le bois sombre des meubles contraste avec les tons de beige, de sable et d'écru. Je conseille une des Suites Junior situées dans les coins des étages supérieurs et qui offrent une vue imprenable sur la Méditerranée et sur la ville – jusqu'à la Sagrada Família et la remarquable Torre Agbar en forme d'ogive dessinée par Jean Nouvel et qui est l'un des gratte-ciel les plus hauts de Barcelone.

Rates: Single and double rooms from 385 €, suites from 500 €, apartments from 1,300 €. Breakfast 28 € (this is included in the rates for apartments).
Rooms: 483 rooms, suites and apartments.
Cuisine: Five restaurants, all specialising in Mediterranean dishes.
History: Opened in 1992, refurbished in 2004.
X-Factor: The spa is on the 42nd and 43rd floors – the terrific view is included in the price of the massage.
Internet: 20 € for 24 hours (high-speed, cable, WLAN).

Preise: EZ/DZ ab 385 €, Suite ab 500 €, Apartment ab 1300 €. Frühstück 28 € (nur inbegriffen bei Apartments).
Zimmer: 483 Zimmer, Suiten und Apartments.
Küche: Fünf Restaurants, die sich auf mediterrane Gerichte spezialisiert haben.
Geschichte: 1992 eröffnet, 2004 renoviert.
X-Faktor: Das Spa liegt im 42. und 43. Stock – die Panoramen sind im Massagepreis inklusive.
Internet: 24 Stunden 20 € (highspeed, Kabel und WLAN).

Prix : Chambre simple ou double à partir de 385 €, suite à partir de 500 €, appartement à partir de 1300 €. Petit déjeuner 28 € (compris dans les appartements).
Chambres : 483 chambres, suites et appartements.
Restauration : Cinq restaurants spécialisés dans la cuisine méditerranéenne.
Histoire : Ouvert en 1992, rénové en 2004.
Le « petit plus » : Le spa est situé au 42e et au 43e étage – le panorama est compris dans le prix du massage.
Internet : 24 heures 20 € (haut débit, câble et WLAN).

1

2

3

1 Cervecería & tapas bar/Cervecería & Tapas-Bar/Cervecería & Bar à tapas

Cervecería El Vaso de Oro
Carrer de Balboa 6
08003 Barcelona
Tel: +34 93 319 30 98
Daily 8am–midnight
Metro: L4 Barceloneta

This tapas bar with a maritime touch, popular with the locals, is situated in La Barceloneta, the former fisherman's quarter. It has an unusually large choice of beers for Barcelona – and they're all a perfect match with the excellent tapas. My ideal evening here starts with a cool "cerveza", followed by some little snacks, and supper in Agua (Passeig Marítim 30, Tel: +34 93 225 12 72) – fantastic!

Diese maritim angehauchte Tapas-Bar im ehemaligen Fischerviertel Barceloneta ist bei Einheimischen sehr beliebt. Sie hat eine für Barcelona einzigartig große Auswahl an Bieren, die hervorragend zu den exzellenten Tapas passen. Mein perfekter Abend sieht hier so aus: Ich trinke eine kühle „cerveza", bestelle ein paar Snacks und gehe anschließend im Agua (Passeig Marítim 30, Tel: +34 93 225 12 72) dinieren – wunderbar!

Situé dans l'ancien quartier de pêcheurs La Barceloneta, ce bar à tapas à l'atmosphère marine est très aimé des habitants. Son grand choix de bières qui s'accordent remarquablement aux excellentes tapas est unique en son genre à Barcelone. Pour moi une soirée parfaite ressemble à ça : boire une « cerveza » bien fraîche », commander un snack et aller ensuite dîner à l' « Agua » (Passeig Marítim 30, Tel: +34 93 225 12 72). La vie est belle !

2 Paella restaurant/Paella-Restaurant/ Restaurant à paella

Restaurant 7 Portes
Passeig d'Isabel II 14
08003 Barcelona
Tel: +34 93 319 30 33
www.7portes.com

Daily 1pm–1am
Metro: L4 Barceloneta

7 Portes is the oldest restaurant in town and a legend (perhaps it could be compared with Zurich's Kronenhalle, equally famous, equally beloved). It opened its "seven doors" in 1836 and today is one of the few middle-class restaurants with a classic interior and formally dressed waiters. Try the Paella "Parellada", named after the head of the gastronomy dynasty, or the superb seafood platters. Famous guests have frequented 7 Portes, of course, but there are no plaques to show the favourite seats of Picasso, Dalí, Orson Welles, Maria Callas or Che Guevara.

7 Portes ist das älteste Restaurant der Stadt und eine Legende (sozusagen die „Kronenhalle" von Barcelona). Es hat seine „sieben Türen" seit 1836 geöffnet und präsentiert sich heute als eines der wenigen bürgerlichen Lokale mit klassischem Interieur und förmlich gekleideten Kellnern, die eine Paella „Parellada" servieren – benannt nach dem Stammvater der Gastronomiedynastie. Sehr lecker sind auch die Meeresfrüchteplatten. Im 7 Portes saßen schon berühmte Gäste: Kleine Plaketten zeigen die einstigen Lieblingsplätze von Picasso, Dalí, Orson Welles, Maria Callas und sogar Che Guevara an.

« 7 Portes » est une légende à Barcelone. Ouvert en 1836, le plus ancien restaurant de la ville est resté l'un des rares établissements bourgeois dotés d'un intérieur classique où des serveurs en livrée servent une paella « Parellada » – nommée d'après le fondateur de la dynastie de restaurateurs. Il faut goûter les plateaux de fruits de mer. Le « 7 Portes » a vu défiler des gens célèbres : des plaquettes indiquent l'endroit où Picasso, Dalí, Orson Welles, Maria Callas et même Che Guevara aimaient s'asseoir.

3 Handmade sweets/Hausgemachte Bonbons/Bonbons maison

Papabubble
Carrer Ample 28
08002 Barcelona
Tel: +34 93 268 86 25

www.papabubble.com
Tues–Fri 10am–2pm and 4pm–8.30pm, Sat 10am–8.30pm, Sun 11am–7.30pm
Metro: L3 Drassanes; L4 Jaume I

These sweets are tiny, whimsical works of art and it is actually a shame to eat them. You can buy them shaped like a toothbrush with green and white striped toothpaste (a good way to persuade the kids to clean their teeth), or as coloured lollipops with the words "Fuck Bush". All the sweets are made in house from sugar and make delicious souvenirs for the young and the young at heart.

Diese Bonbons sind witzige kleine Kunstwerke und eigentlich viel zu schade zum Essen. Es gibt sie zum Beispiel in Form von Zahnbürsten mit grün-weiß gestreifter Zahnpasta (so bringt man dem Nachwuchs das Zähneputzen bei) oder als bunte Lollis mit der Aufschrift „Fuck Bush". Alle Süßigkeiten werden direkt im Laden aus Zucker hergestellt – leckere Souvenirs für kleine und große Kinder.

À vrai dire ces minuscules œuvres d'art sont trop belles pour être mangées. On les trouve sous forme de brosse à dents couverte de dentifrice rayé blanc-vert (rien de tels pour apprendre aux petits à se brosser les dents) ou sous forme de sucette avec l'inscription « Fuck Bush ». Toutes les douceurs sont fabriquées en sucre dans la boutique – des souvenirs délicieux pour les enfants, petits et grands.

4 Sweet restaurant/Süßes Restaurant/ Restaurant sucré

Espai Sucre
Carrer de la Princesa 53
08003 Barcelona
Tel: +34 93 268 16 30
www.espaisucre.com
Tues–Sat 9pm–11.30pm
Metro: L4 Jaume I

The inventive talent of the Catalans is boundless, and they certainly know how to use it to satisfy their sweet tooth. No other city in the world is as mad about chocolate and sugar as Barcelona! At least, I have

4

© akg-images / Hilbich

5

6

never seen a restaurant like Espai Sucre anywhere else. Here, desserts are served as three or six-course meals – if you want little savory dishes, you must order them as a prelude to the sweet main event. Pretty eccentric, I'd say. And that is why you shouldn't miss it.

Der Erfindergeist der Katalanen ist groß, ihr Zahn süß – Barcelona gehört mit Sicherheit zu den schokolade- und zucker-verrücktesten Städten der Welt. Ein Restaurant wie das Espai Sucre habe ich zumindest noch nirgendwo sonst gesehen: Hier werden Süßspeisen als drei- oder sechsgängige Hauptmenüs angeboten (lediglich als Auftakt kann man herzhafte Kleinigkeiten bekommen). Nicht ganz normal, und genau deshalb sollte man es sich nicht entgehen lassen.

Les catalans ont l'esprit inventif et le palais sucré – Barcelone est sûrement une des villes les plus folles de chocolat et de su-creries. En tout cas je n'ai vu nulle part de restaurant comme « Espai Sucre ». On offre ici des menus sucrés de trois à six plats (les petits plats salés ne sont qu'un prélude). Cela sort vraiment de l'ordinaire, et c'est bien pour cette raison qu'il faut y aller.

---

5   Catalan architecture/Katalanische
     Architektur/Architecture catalane

Palau de la Música Catalana
Carrer del Palau de la Música 4-6
08003 Barcelona
Tel: + 34 93 295 72 00
http://home.palaumusica.org
Daily 10am–3.30pm
Metro: L1, L4 Urquinaona

This is one important building in Barcelona not designed by Gaudí, but by the other great Catalan architect, Lluís Domènech i Montaner. It was constructed in 1908 as a concert hall for Catalan music, and in 1997 was declared a UNESCO World Heritage Site. Montaner personally designed every detail inside and out. It is a symphony of mosaics, busts, sculptures and columns, vibrant-tiled decorations, curved staircases and ornate ceilings. The giddy designs are as eccentric as anything turned out by

Gaudí. I find the huge coloured glass drop on the ceiling of the concert hall especially spectacular.

Ein wichtiger Bau in Barcelona, der nicht von Gaudí entworfen wurde, sondern von dem anderen großen katalanischen Archi-tekten, Lluís Domènech i Montaner. Er errichtete ihn 1908 als Konzerthalle für katalanische Musik – 1997 ernannte die UNESCO das Werk zum Weltkulturerbe. Montaner hat das Innere und Äußere bis ins Detail persönlich gestaltet. Es ist eine Sinfonie aus Mosaiken, Büsten, Skulpturen sowie Säulen, lebhaften Fliesendekors, geschwungenen Treppen und mit Orna-menten überzogenen Decken, deren Exzentrik selbst von Gaudí nicht übertroffen wurde. Besonders spektakulär finde ich den riesigen Buntglastropfen an der Decke des Konzertsaals.

Ce bâtiment emblématique à Barcelone n'a pas été construit par Gaudí mais par un autre grand architecte catalan, Lluís Domènech i Montaner. Édifié en 1908, le Palais de la Musique Catalane a été déclaré « Patrimoine de l'humanité » par l'UNESCO en 1997. Montaner a veillé per-sonnellement sur la décoration intérieure et extérieure. C'est une symphonie de mosaïques, de bustes, de statues et de colonnes, de carrelages aux décors exubé-rants, d'escaliers en volute et de plafonds ornementés – même Gaudí ne sut faire plus excentrique. Spectaculaire : l'imposante goutte de verre coloré au plafond de la salle de concert.

---

6   Open-air cinema/Open-Air-Kino/
     Cinéma de plein air

Sala Montjuïc
Next to Castell de Montjuïc (Sala M)
info@salamontjuic.com
www.salamontjuic.com
July and August. Buses take you to the cinema (8.30pm–9.30pm, from Torres de la Plaça Espanya) and bring you back after the film. *(Map on page 192/193)*

A visit to an open-air cinema is one of summer's great pleasures. Such an evening is even better if the cinema is

located right at the seaside and a warm breeze gently strokes your hair as you watch the film. In the Sala Montjuïc you don't sit in a hall, as the name would lead you to expect – you lie on the grass in a picnic meadow. Don't forget to bring something to eat and drink. The films, shown in the original with Spanish sub-titles, are projected onto the solid walls of the Castell de Montjuïc. They start after sunset, at around 10.15pm.

Eines der großen Sommervergnügen ist der Besuch eines Freiluftkinos – noch schöner sind solche Abende, wenn das Kino nahe am Meer liegt und man beim Zuschauen von der warmen Brise um-schmeichelt wird. In der Sala Montjuïc sitzt man, anders als der Name vermuten lässt, nicht in einem Saal, sondern liegt auf einer Picknick-Wiese (Essen und Getränke bitte selbst mitbringen). Die Filme im Original mit spanischen Untertiteln werden an eine Leinwand an den massiven Mauern des Castell de Montjuïc projiziert – Beginn ist nach Sonnenuntergang um 22.15 Uhr.

Voir un film en plein air est l'un des grands plaisir estivaux. Et ces soirées sont plus belles encore quand le cinéma se trouve près de la mer et que l'on est éventé par une brise tiède. Son nom ne l'indique pas, mais dans la Sala Montjuïc, on est assis sur une prairie où chacun peut apporter son pique-nique. Les films en version originale avec sous-titres espagnols sont projetés sur un écran tendu sur les murs massifs du Castell de Montjuïc – début vers 22h15, après le coucher du soleil.

Personal discoveries/Eigene
Entdeckungen/Découvertes personnelles :

_____

_____

_____

_____

_____

_____

1 Church & architecture/Kirche & Architektur/
Église & architecture
Sagrada Família

2 Classic tapas/Klassische Tapas/Tapas classiques
TapaÇ24

3 Travel books/Reiseliteratur/Livres de voyage
Llibreria Altaïr

4 Flowers around the clock/24-Stunden-Blumen/Fleurs 24h/24
Floristería Navarro

5 Club, bar & café/Club, Bar & Café/Club, bar & café
Mond Bar & Cafè del Sol

---

1 Films in their original language/Filme im Original/
Films en version originale
Verdi 5 Salas Barcelona

2 Wine & more/Wein & more/Vins & plus
D.O.

3 Spanish ham/Spanischer Schinken/Jambon d'Espagne
Charcuterías Joaquín Gracia

4 Lunch/Mittagessen/Déjeuner
Valentín

5 Chocolate/Schokolade/Chocolats
Oriol Balaguer

---

1 Museum & architecture/Museum & Architektur/
Musée & architecture
Fundació Antoni Tàpies

2 Tapas bar/Tapas-Bar/Bar à tapas
Bar Mut

3 Photography books & gallery/Fotografie-Bücher & Galerie/
Livres de photographie & galerie
Kowasa

4 Spanish restaurant/Spanisches Restaurant/
Restaurant espagnol
Flash Flash Tortillería

5 Spanish fashion/Spanische Mode/Mode espagnole
Josep Font

---

1 Architecture & concerts/Architektur & Konzerte/
Architecture & concerts
Casa Milà (La Pedrera)

2 Tea salon & more/Teesalon & more/Salon de thé & plus
Farga

3 Furniture & more/Möbel & more/Mobilier & plus
Coriumcasa

4 Legendary design shop/Legendärer Designshop/
Designshop légendaire
Vinçon

5 Cervecería/Cervecería/Cervecería
Cervecería Catalana

L'Eixample

128 Hostal Oliva
138 Hostal Girona
146 Hotel Omm
156 987 Barcelona Hotel

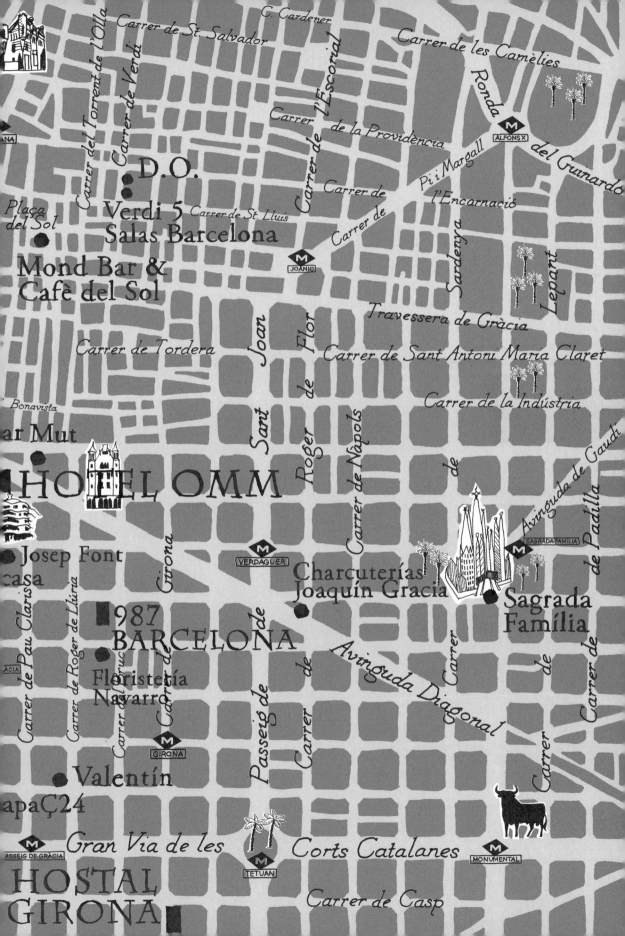

Hostal Oliva

Passeig de Gràcia, 32   08007 Barcelona
☎ +34 93 488 01 62   ☐ +34 93 487 04 97
hostaloliva@lasguias.com
www.hostaloliva.com
Metro: L2, L3, L4 Passeig de Gràcia
Booking: www.great-escapes-hotels.com

Hostal Oliva

This little guest house is located diagonally opposite Gaudí's famous Casa Batlló on the Passeig de Gràcia. In spite of its bustling location, the hotel's rooms are pleasantly quiet, since they're on the top floor of a four-storey corner house built in 1871. You might think you've walked into the wrong house when you see the stately staircase with its wrought-iron banister, the black-and-white tiled floor and old columns. It's a grand ambience you don't usually associate with a little guest house. The original old lift takes you up to the "hostal". The rooms are clean, airy, sweet-smelling, and still have the original Spanish Art-Déco furniture (the hostel opened in 1931). Even though designer hotels are popping up everywhere in Barcelona, you'd be hard-pressed to find a more stylish place to stay. The new hotels may be immaculate, modern and well located, like the nearby Hostal Goya. But Hostal Oliva has more charm and atmosphere by far.

Direkt gegenüber dem Passeig de Gràcia und schräg gegenüber von Gaudís berühmter Casa Batlló liegt diese kleine Pension. Trotz der belebten, zentralen Straße ist sie ruhig, denn sie befindet sich im vierten und obersten Stock eines Eckgebäudes aus dem Jahr 1871. Beim Betreten des hochherrschaftlichen Treppenhauses mit gusseisernen Geländern, schwarz-weiß gefliestem Boden und alten Säulen meint man zunächst, an der falschen Adresse zu sein, da man ja eine kleine Pension sucht – doch ein Originalaufzug aus Holz fährt hinauf zum Hostal. Die Wohnung ist sauber, hell und wohlriechend, dazu kommt, dass die Zimmer mit original spanischen Art-déco-Möbeln aus den 1920ern ausgestattet sind (das Hostal wurde 1931 eröffnet). Stylischer lässt es sich in Barcelona kaum wohnen – selbst wenn hier überall designte Herbergen aus dem Boden sprießen und zum Teil tadellos, modern und gut gelegen sind (wie das nahe Hostal Goya). Aber das Hostal Oliva besitzt um Welten mehr Charme und Atmosphäre.

Située presque en face du Casa Batlló de Gaudí, cette petite pension se trouve sur le Passeig de Gràcia. Malgré l'animation de cette artère commerçante, l'hôtel est calme car il se trouve au quatrième et dernier étage d'un immeuble en coin datant de 1871. En pénétrant dans la somptueuse cage d'escalier avec sa rampe en fonte, son carrelage en noir et blanc et ses anciennes colonnes, vous aurez d'abord l'impression de vous être trompé d'adresse, mais un authentique ascenseur vous conduira effectivement à la petite pension propre et claire. Le mobilier des chambres est de style art déco espagnol des années 1920 (l'hôtel a ouvert en 1931). Difficile de résider avec plus de style à Barcelone, même si les hôtels design poussent ici comme des champignons et qu'une bonne partie d'entre eux sont modernes et bien situés (comme l'« Hostal Goya » non loin de là). Mais l'Hostal Oliva a beaucoup plus de charme.

Rates: Single rooms with washbasin, 36 €, double rooms with washbasin, 60 €, double rooms with en-suite bathroom, 75 €.
Rooms: 16 rooms.
Cuisine: The "hostal" does not serve breakfast, lunch or supper. But there are plenty of bars and restaurants nearby.
History: Opened in 1931.
X-Factor: The friendly staff will give you helpful sightseeing tips.
Internet: Not available.

Preise: EZ mit Waschbecken 36 €, DZ mit Waschbecken 60 €, DZ mit Bad 75 €.
Zimmer: 16 Zimmer.
Küche: Das Hostal bietet weder einen Frühstücksservice noch Mittag- oder Abendessen. In der unmittelbaren Umgebung gibt es aber zahlreiche Bars und Restaurants.
Geschichte: 1931 eröffnet.
X-Faktor: Das Personal verrät gerne die besten Tipps fürs Sightseeing in Barcelona.
Internet: Nicht vorhanden.

Prix : Chambre simple avec lavabo 36 €, chambre double avec lavabo 60 €, chambre double avec salle de bains 75 €.
Chambres : 16 chambres.
Restauration : Non proposée. Toutefois, vous trouverez à proximité une multitude de bars et de restaurants.
Histoire : Ouvert en 1931.
Le « petit plus » : Le personnel vous indiquera volontiers les meilleurs endroits à visiter dans Barcelone.
Internet : Non disponible.

1

2

3

1 Church & architecture/Kirche &
Architektur/Église & architecture

Sagrada Família
Carrer de Mallorca 401
08013 Barcelona
Tel: +34 93 207 30 31
www.sagradafamilia.org
October–March 9am–6pm,
April–September 9am–8pm
Metro: L2, L5 Sagrada Família

The Sagrada Família is to Barcelona what
Notre Dame is to Paris and the Cathedral
is to Cologne. Like these other great land-
marks, the Sagrada Familia has taken a
long time to build. Gaudí began construction of his masterpiece more than 100 years
ago, in 1883. The cathedral's completion
date is still uncertain. (After all, Cologne
Cathedral took more than 600 years.)
In the meantime, both the façade and
the crypt were declared UNESCO World
Heritage Sites in 2005.

Was der Dom für Köln ist, ist die Sagrada
Família für Barcelona. Die beiden Wahrzeichen eint eine lange Bauzeit – für den Kölner Dom benötigte man mehr als 600 Jahre,
mit der Sagrada Família begann Gaudí vor
über 100 Jahren (1883) – und das Datum
der Vollendung steht noch nicht fest. Doch
bereits 2005 erklärte die UNESCO die Fassade sowie die Krypta zum Weltkulturerbe.

La Sagrada Família est pour Barcelone ce
que le Kölner Dom est pour Cologne. Ces
deux symboles de leur ville respective ont
en commun une durée de construction particulièrement longue : plus de six cents ans
pour la cathédrale de Cologne et plus d'un
siècle pour la Sagrada Família commencée
par Gaudí en 1883. La date d'achèvement
de cette dernière n'est d'ailleurs pas encore fixée. Mais ceci n'a pas empêché
l'UNESCO de classer en 2005 la façade
et la crypte au patrimoine mondial.

2 Classic tapas/Klassische Tapas/
Tapas classiques

TapaÇ24
Carrer de la Diputació 269

08007 Barcelona
Tel: +34 93 488 09 77
www.carlesabellan.com
Mon–Sat 8am–midnight
Metro: L2, L3, L4 Passeig de Gràcia

To get to this restaurant, take a few steps
down into the basement, where a tiled floor,
stand-up bistro tables and neon lighting
creates a pretty uninviting atmosphere.
But looks are misleading. Here the service
is speedy and straightforward, the tapas
menu on the wall short and filled with the
classics. Everything here is absolutely
fresh and really delicious. If you're in search
of top-quality dishes served in an unfussy
setting, and aren't in the mood either for a
pseudo-designer environment or folksy
cuteness, then this is the place for you. Try
to find out what is behind "Bikini Ç24"!

Ein paar Stufen führen hinunter ins
Souterrain, wo Fliesenboden, Stehtische
und Neonröhren ein fast etwas ungemüt-
liches Flair verbreiten. Der Service ist
schnell und schnörkellos, die Tapas-Karte
an Wandtafeln übersichtlich und klassisch
– und alles ist hier superfrisch und köstlich.
Wer unprätentiöse Atmosphäre sowie hohe
Qualität schätzt und sich nicht so gerne in
krampfhaftem Designambiente oder in
Folklorebuden aufhält, ist hier goldrichtig.
Versuchen Sie herauszufinden, was sich
hinter „Bikini Ç24" verbirgt!

Quelques marches vous conduiront au
sous-sol où le sol en carrelage, les tables
sans chaises et les tubes néon donnent à
ce bar un aspect presque inhospitalier. Le
service est rapide, la carte de tapas inscrite
sur le tableau au mur est concise et classique. Ici, les tapas sont tous très frais et
succulents. Vous êtes à la bonne adresse,
si vous appréciez la qualité et la simplicité
et si vous ne recherchez pas les établissements folkloriques ou ceux qui se veulent
design à tout prix. Essayez donc de décou-
vrir ce qui se cache derrière « Bikini Ç24 » !

3 Travel books/Reiseliteratur/Livres
de voyage

Llibreria Altaïr
Gran Via de les Corts Catalanes 616

(between Carrer de Balmes & Rambla
de Catalunya)
08007 Barcelona
Tel: +34 93 342 71 71
www.altair.es
Mon–Sat 10am–2pm and 4.30pm–8.30pm
Metro: L1, L2 Universitat; L2, L3, L4
Passeig de Gràcia

There are only a handful of bookstores
in the world that have such a terrific and
extensive selection of travel books. Here
you'll find everything and anything related
to travel-literary works, maps and guide-
books, and volumes of geography, anthro-
pology and nature from every corner of the
planet. There's even a special department
with cookery books from all over the world.
Here, in a very small space, you can feel
how huge, rich, varied and wonderful our
planet is. I find it a fascinating place.

Es gibt weltweit nur wenige Buchläden, die
sich so intensiv auf Reiseliteratur inklusive
Karten und Führer sowie auf Titel rund um
Reisen, Anthropologie und Natur bis in
den kleinsten Winkel dieser Erde spezialisiert haben. Dieses Geschäft besitzt sogar
eine eigene Abteilung mit Kochbüchern
aus aller Welt. Hier kann man auf wenigen
Quadratmetern erfahren, wie groß, reich-
haltig, vielfältig und wunderbar unser
Planet ist – für mich einfach faszinierend.

Il existe à travers le monde peu de librai-
ries aussi spécialisées dans la littérature
de voyage (plans et guides compris) et
dans les livres sur l'anthropologie, la nature
et les contrées les plus reculées de notre
planète. Ce magasin possède même un
emplacement entièrement consacré aux
livres de cuisine de tous les pays. Sur
quelques mètres carrés on découvre ici
combien la Terre est grande, diversifiée
et magnifique – une chose pour moi tout
simplement fascinante.

4 Flowers around the clock/24-Stunden-
Blumen/Fleurs 24h/24

Floristería Navarro
Carrer de València 320
08009 Barcelona
Tel: +34 93 207 36 61

4

5

www.floristeriasnavarro.com
Open 24/7
Metro: L4 Girona; L4, L5 Verdaguer

A bouquet of fresh, fragrant flowers can turn a strange hotel room into a comfy home away from home. Navarro is a lovely option for travellers who plan to stay longer than two days in a hotel, or who have booked into a simple guest house like Hostal Oliva, where no flowers are put in the rooms. This big shop (800 square metres) is like a flower supermarket, and it's open 24 hours a day (every town should have one!). They even have fruit baskets arranged like a bouquet – you can eat the "flowers" before you leave your hotel.

Wenn man ein Hotel länger als zwei Tage bezieht oder in einer einfacheren Pension wie dem Hostal Oliva reserviert, wo für die Gäste keine Blumen hingestellt werden, schafft Navarro Abhilfe. Mit einem Strauß frischer, am besten duftender Schnittblumen lässt sich in fremden Zimmern im Handumdrehen eine schönere Atmosphäre schaffen. Der Clou ist, dass dieser 800 Quadratmeter große Laden 24 Stunden am Tag geöffnet hat – so etwas würde ich mir in jeder Stadt wünschen. Es gibt hier auch wie Blumensträuße arrangierte Obstkörbe – die kann man sogar noch vor der Abreise aufessen.

Si les fleurs vous manquent parce que vous résidez plus de deux jours dans un hôtel ou parce que vous avez réservé une chambre dans une pension toute simple comme le Hostal Oliva, vous pouvez alors faire appel à Navarro. Avec un bouquet de fleurs, votre chambre d'hôtel vous semblera tout de suite plus accueillante et vous vous sentirez comme chez vous. Le magasin de huit cents mètre carrés a en plus l'avantage d'être ouvert 24 heures sur 24, et il propose des corbeilles de fruits que vous pourrez déguster avant votre départ.

5   Club, bar & café/Club, Bar & Café/
     Club, bar & café

Mond Bar & Cafè del Sol
Plaça del Sol 21 & 16
08012 Barcelona

Tel: +34 93 272 09 10 (Mond Bar)
Tel: +34 93 415 56 63 (Cafè del Sol)
www.mondclub.com
Mond Bar is open daily from 8.30pm; Cafè del Sol is open Tues–Sun midday–2am
Metro: L3 Fontana

The idyllic, paved Plaça del Sol is at its best on balmy summer evenings and warm nights. It has its own special flair and is certainly worth a visit. Cafè del Sol and the Mond Bar are both ideal meeting places for young and old, and have sidewalk tables. Everybody in Barcelona knows the Mond Bar.

Vor allem an lauen Sommerabenden und in warmen Nächten kommt der Charme der idyllischen, gepflasterten Plaça del Sol zur Geltung – sie hat ein ganz eigenes Flair und lohnt unbedingt einen Besuch. Ideale Treffpunkte für Jung und Alt sind das Cafè del Sol sowie die Mond Bar, die beide Tische unter freiem Himmel aufstellen. Außerdem ist die Mond Bar ein stadtbekannter Club.

Revêtue de pavés, l'idyllique Plaça del Sol est particulièrement agréable les nuits d'été. Avec son atmosphère incomparable, elle vaut vraiment le détour. Lieux de rencontre pour jeunes et moins jeunes, le Cafè del Sol et le Mond Bar dressent leurs tables sur la place quand il fait beau. Le Mond Bar est par ailleurs un club réputé de Barcelone.

Personal discoveries/Eigene Entdeckungen/Découvertes personnelles :

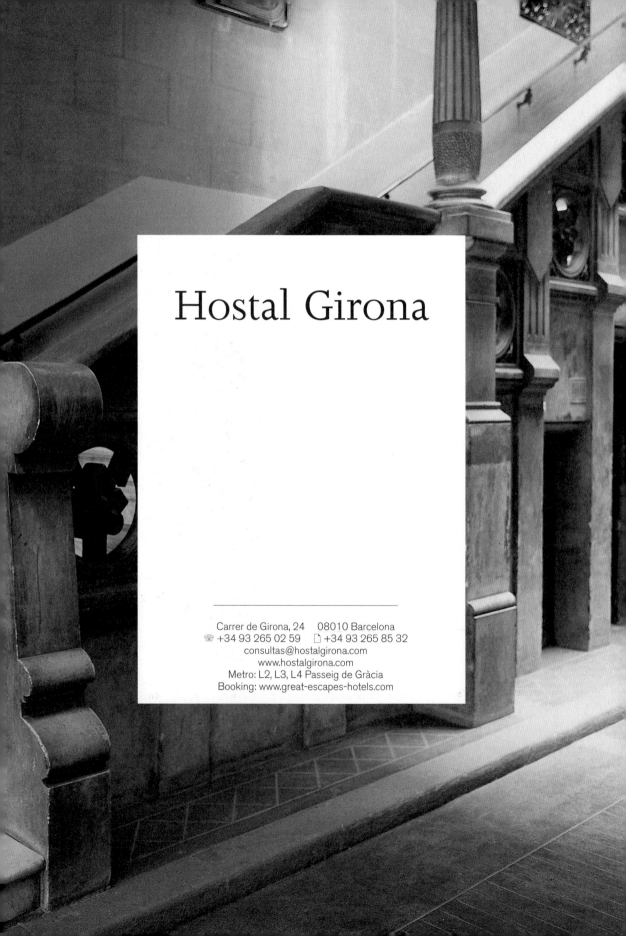

Hostal Girona

Carrer de Girona, 24   08010 Barcelona
☎ +34 93 265 02 59   📠 +34 93 265 85 32
consultas@hostalgirona.com
www.hostalgirona.com
Metro: L2, L3, L4 Passeig de Gràcia
Booking: www.great-escapes-hotels.com

Hostal Girona

This impressive building, designed by Ildefons Cerdà, was constructed in the heart of bourgeois Eixample in the 19th century. It's close to the Passeig de Gràcia, where both of Gaudí's civil buildings, Casa Batlló and Casa Milà, are located. The entrance to this little guest house is very grand indeed. Sweeping staircases with stone balustrades and pillars on each side of the patio lead up to the "hostal" on the first floor. I've never seen a more impressive entrance. The "hostal" is an apartment with a typically Spanish layout and is completely furnished with antiques. Two incredibly long corridors with windows overlooking the patio lead to the rooms, which feature antique wooden furniture. The rooms radiate an authenticity that comes partly from the classic white bed linen and cotton and linen covers (you don't see that very often!), and partly from the unusually elaborate tile floors. I love this flair, unique in designer-obsessed Barcelona.

Das eindrucksvolle Gebäude wurde von Ildefons Cerdà entworfen und im 19. Jahrhundert im Herzen des bourgeoisen Eixample errichtet, nahe des Passeig de Gràcia, wo auch Gaudís Wohnbauten Casa Batlló und Casa Milà stehen. Der Eingang zur kleinen Pension ist wahnsinnig imposant: Rechts und links führen im Patio zwei monumentale Treppen zum Hostal im ersten Geschoss – die Stufen sind erhaben und mit steinernen Balustraden und Säulen versehen; ich habe noch nie ein vergleichbar eindrucksvolles Entree gesehen. Das Hostal ist eine typisch spanisch geschnittene Wohnung, die komplett mit Antiquitäten eingerichtet wurde. Zwei ellenlange Korridore mit Fenstern zum Patio führen zu den Zimmern, in denen antike Holzmöbel stehen. Klassisch weißes Bettzeug, Überdecken aus Leinen und Baumwolle (gibt es nur noch ganz selten!), und vor allem die außergewöhnlich elaborierten alten Fliesenböden verleihen den Räumen ein authentisches Flair – für mich in dieser Art einzigartig im manchmal überdesignten Barcelona.

Dessiné par Ildefons Cerdà, l'imposant immeuble a été édifié au XIXe siècle en plein cœur du quartier bourgeois L'Eixample, non loin du Passeig de Gràcia, où se trouvent aussi les bâtiments civils de Gaudí, la Casa Batlló et la Casa Milà. L'entrée de la petite pension est stupéfiante : à droite et à gauche dans le patio, deux escaliers monumentaux conduisent à l'Hostal au premier étage. Les marches sont spacieuses et encadrées de balustrades et de colonnes en pierre. Personnellement je n'ai encore jamais vu une entrée aussi impressionnante. Entièrement décoré avec des antiquités, l'Hostal a une répartition de ses pièces typiquement espagnole. Deux interminables couloirs ponctués de fenêtres donnant sur le patio mènent aux chambres, lesquelles sont aménagées de meubles anciens. Les draps blancs classiques, les dessus de lit en lin et coton (qui se font de plus en plus rares !) et surtout les vieux carrelages au sol confèrent aux chambres un caractère authentique, tout à fait exceptionnel dans ce Barcelone parfois trop design.

Rates: Single rooms 35 €–45 €, double rooms 58 €–75 € (some of the rooms don't have en-suite bathrooms).
Rooms: 20 rooms.
Cuisine: The "hostal" does not serve breakfast, lunch or supper. However, there are several good bars and restaurants along the same street.
History: The building dates from 1860.
X-Factor: The familial atmosphere – you have the feeling that you are at home in Barcelona.
Internet: Not available.

Preise: EZ 35–45 €, DZ 58–75 € (nicht alle Zimmer haben ein eigenes Bad).
Zimmer: 20 Zimmer.
Küche: Das Hostal serviert weder Frühstück noch Mittag- oder Abendessen. Direkt in der Carrer de Girona gibt es aber mehrere gute Bars und Restaurants.
Geschichte: Hier residiert man in einem Haus aus dem Jahr 1860.
X-Faktor: Die familiäre Atmosphäre – es ist fast so, als ob man in Barcelona leben würde.
Internet: Nicht vorhanden.

Prix : Chambre simple 35–45 €, chambre double 58–75 € (toutes les chambres n'ont pas une salle de bains).
Chambres : 20 chambres.
Restauration : Non proposée. Nombreux bars et restaurants à proximité.
Histoire : Vous résiderez dans une maison datant de 1860.
Le « petit plus » : L'ambiance familiale, vous n'aurez pas l'impression d'être étranger.
Internet : Non disponible.

1   Films in their original language/Filme im Original/Films en version originale

Verdi 5 Salas Barcelona
Carrer de Verdi 32
08012 Barcelona
Tel: +34 93 238 79 90
www.cines-verdi.com
Metro: L3 Fontana; L4 Joanic

It's always better to watch films in their original language, and that's especially true if you don't speak Spanish (a lot of the foreign films screened in Barcelona are dubbed). This cinema shows an excellent selection of good international productions. It's an ideal way to pass the time before going out to supper, which is never before 9pm (and often more like 10pm) in Barcelona.

Am besten sieht man sich immer Filme im Original an – vor allem aber, wenn man kein Spanisch spricht. In diesem Kino wird eine ausgezeichnete Auswahl an guten Produktionen angeboten. Ein idealer Zeitvertreib vor dem Abendessen, da man in Barcelona auf keinen Fall vor 21 Uhr ausgeht, eher sogar 22 Uhr.

Il vaut toujours mieux regarder un film dans sa version originale, et à fortiori si on ne sait pas l'espagnol. Ce cinéma propose un excellent choix de films. Un moyen idéal pour passer le temps avant d'aller dîner car on ne sort en aucun cas à Barcelone avant 21 heures, voire même 22 heures.

2   Wine & more/Wein & more/Vins & plus

D.O.
Carrer de Verdi 36
08012 Barcelona
Tel: +34 93 218 96 73
Daily 6pm–2am
Metro: L3 Fontana; L4 Joanic

This tiny, seven-table restaurant and bar (expect to wait) specialises in fine wines. The excellent tapas served with the different wines are always just right. Specialities include "croquetas de jamón" (ham croquettes) and delicious Catalan olives.

Dieses winzige Restaurant mit nur sieben Tischen und einer Bar (bitte Wartezeit einplanen) hat sich auf hervorragende Weine spezialisiert. Zu den ausgewählten Sorten werden ausgezeichnete und immer passende Tapas, Spezialitäten wie „croquetas de jamón" (Schinkenkroketten) oder köstliche katalanische Oliven serviert.

Ce minuscule restaurant, qui ne comporte que sept tables et un bar (prévoyez de l'attente), s'est spécialisé dans les bons vins. Pour accompagner ces excellents crus, on vous servira de délicieux tapas, des spécialités comme les « croquetas de jamón » (croquettes de jambon) ou de succulentes olives catalanes.

3   Spanish ham/Spanischer Schinken/Jambon d'Espagne

Charcuterías Joaquín Gracia
Avinguda Diagonal 366
08018 Barcelona
Tel: +34 93 458 05 76
Daily 8.30am–2pm and 5pm–9pm
Metro: L4, L5 Verdaguer

The range of Spanish hams is enormous. Every region produces its own speciality. The best ham is "pata negra" – or "jamón ibérico" – which is produced from the rare, black-hoofed Iberian pigs fed exclusively on a diet of acorns. Or ask for delicious Serrano ham, preferably of bellota quality. In Joaquín Gracia's "charcuteria", numerous sides of ham hang from the walls and the ceiling, or are on display in glass cabinets. It looks very much like a film set or a painting. There is no more authentic way to buy this delicious souvenir, but you can also pick up vacuum-packed Spanish ham at the airport.

In Spanien gibt es eine riesige Auswahl an Schinkensorten: Jede Region hat ihre eigene Spezialität. Der beste Schinken ist der „pata negra" – oder „jamón ibérico" –, der vom seltenen iberischen Schwein mit schwarzen Klauen stammt, das nur mit Eicheln gefüttert wird. Oder man bestellt köstlichen Serrano-Schinken; am besten von der Qualitätsstufe „bellota". Bei Joaquín Gracia hängen unzählige Hinterschinken an den Wänden, von der Decke oder liegen hinter Glasvitrinen, das Ganze sieht wie ein Filmset oder Gemälde aus. Authentischer lassen sich die delikaten Souvenirs nicht einkaufen (am Flughafen gibt es z.B. auch vakuumverpackten spanischen Schinken).

Vous trouverez en Espagne un choix considérable de variétés de jambon : chaque région a sa spécialité. Le meilleur jambon est le « pata negra » – ou « jamón ibérico » –, qui provient du cochon noir ibérique, un animal assez rare nourri aux glands de chêne. Vous pourrez aussi commander du jambon serrano, de préférence de qualité « bellota ». Chez Joaquín Gracia un nombre incalculable de jambons sont accrochés aux murs et au plafond, et sont aussi exposés en vitrine. Le tout ressemble à un décor de film ou à un tableau. Impossible d'acheter ces délicieux souvenirs de manière plus couleur locale (à l'aéroport, on vous propose aussi par exemple du jambon espagnol emballé sous vide).

4   Lunch/Mittagessen/Déjeuner

Valentín
Carrer de la Diputació 301
08009 Barcelona
Tel: +34 93 487 23 72
Daily 1pm–4.30pm and 8.30pm–11.30pm
Metro: L2, L3, L4 Passeig de Gràcia

You can choose from two different Catalan set lunches here, and all the dishes are basic, classic and always freshly prepared. The Spanish really savour their long lunch breaks, since they have supper very late. So Valentín's is a meeting place for locals of all different walks of life.

Hier kann man wunderbar aus zwei unterschiedlichen katalanischen Mittagsmenüs wählen – alle Speisen sind klassisch, unkompliziert und immer frisch zubereitet. Auf ihre ausgedehnte Lunchpause legen die Spanier großen Wert, da sie erst sehr spät zu Abend essen. Und so treffen sich

4

5

bei Valentín die Berufstätigen aller Couleur aus dem Viertel.

Pour le déjeuner, vous pourrez choisir ici entre deux menus catalans. Tous les plats sont traditionnels, sobres et préparés sur commande. Les Espagnols aiment que leur repas de midi dure longtemps car ils mangent très tard le soir. Chez « Valentin » on rencontre donc tous ceux qui font leur pause-midi dans le quartier.

5   Chocolate/Schokolade/Chocolats

Oriol Balaguer
Plaça de Sant Gregori Taumaturg 2
08021 Barcelona
Tel: +34 93 201 18 46
www.oriolbalaguer.com
Mon–Sat 10am–2.30pm and 5pm–9pm,
Sun 10am–12.30pm
Metro: L6 La Bonanova, Muntaner

Oriol Balaguer's desserts, cakes and chocolate creations have won all the most important national and international gastronomy prizes. With its nine different flavours and 64%, 70% or 80% cocoa content, his BCN collection is absolutely out of this world, and makes a great souvenir. This outstanding chocolate is packed in beautifully-designed paper that reveals its origins at a glance. A selection of the six best chocolate creations is wrapped like a cocoa bean and is very attractive indeed.

Oriol Balaguer wurde für seine Desserts, Kuchen- und Schokoladekreationen bereits mit den wichtigsten nationalen und internationalen Gastronomiepreisen ausgezeichnet. Seine „BCN Collection" – in neun Geschmacksrichtungen und mit 64, 70 oder 80 Prozent Kakaoanteil – sind köstlich und ein tolles Mitbringsel. Denn diese ausgezeichneten Schokoladen sind in grafisch hervorragend gestaltetem Papier verpackt, das seine Herkunft auf den ersten Blick verrät. Wunderschön ist auch das verpackte Sortiment der sechs besten Schokoladekreationen in Kakaobohnenform.

Oriol Balaguer a déjà remporté les principaux prix nationaux et internationaux

de gastronomie pour ses desserts et ses créations de gâteaux et de chocolats. Sa « BCN Collection », en neuf parfums et avec 64, 70 ou 80 pour cent de cacao, possède un goût divin et vous ferez des heureux en l'offrant. En regardant l'excellent graphisme du papier qui enveloppe ces succulents chocolats, on devine d'emblée leur origine. Le mélange des six meilleures créations de chocolats en forme de fève de cacao est également magnifique.

Personal discoveries/Eigene Entdeckungen/Découvertes personnelles :

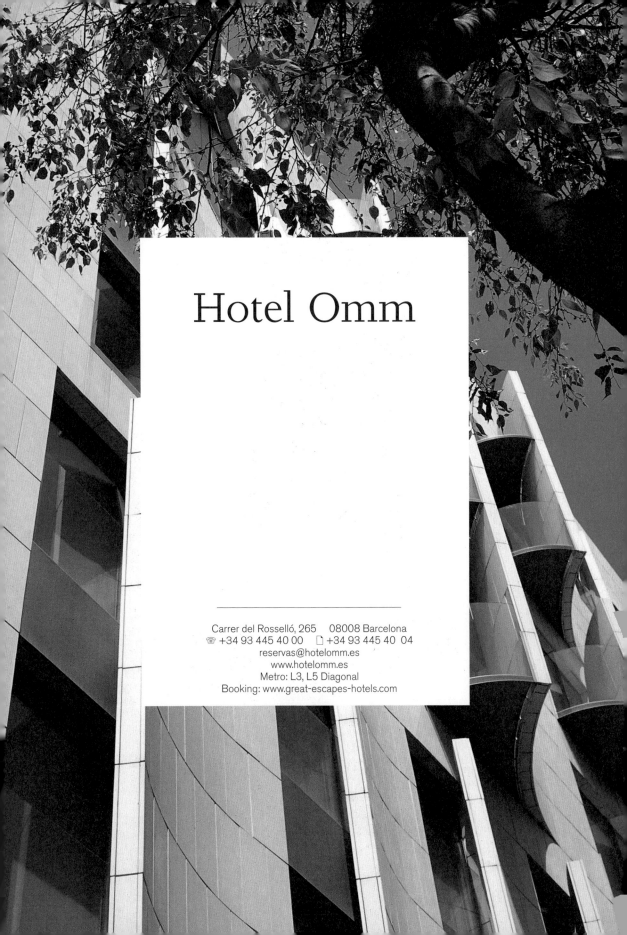

Hotel Omm

Carrer del Rosselló, 265   08008 Barcelona
☎ +34 93 445 40 00   📠 +34 93 445 40 04
reservas@hotelomm.es
www.hotelomm.es
Metro: L3, L5 Diagonal
Booking: www.great-escapes-hotels.com

Hotel Omm

This is the first hotel project from Barcelona's famous restaurateurs, the Tragaluz group, and it's an excellent debut. It's already a hot spot with the international fashion set as well as with Barcelona's hip in-crowd, who lounge on the lobby sofas, or unwind in Arne Jacobsen's "Egg Chair" next to the fireplace. Both restaurants and the Club Ommsession in the basement have rapidly become trendsetters' darlings. The hotel designers have succeeded in creating a harmonious atmosphere that is modern, uncluttered and still cosy. Deep black corridors dimly lit by a strip of floor lighting lead to the rooms. In surprising contrast, the rooms are light and airy. They have been designed in minimalist style with warm colours, wooden flooring and furniture, leather curtains and they're appointed with design classics, like Bertoia's Diamond Armchair. The rooftop terrace and pool afford a fine view stretching from La Pedrera to the sea, as panoramic as anything in a Hollywood film.

Das erste Hotel der Tragaluz-Gruppe, die für ihre exzellenten Restaurants in Barcelona bekannt ist, ist ein gelungener Start. Die internationale Modeszene, aber auch die hippen Barcelonesen gehen hier gerne ein und aus und relaxen auf den Sofas in der Lobby oder im „Egg Chair" von Arne Jacobsen am Kamin. Auch die beiden Restaurants sowie der Club Ommsession im Souterrain sind schnell zum Mekka der Trendsetter geworden. Die Designer des Hotels haben es geschafft, eine harmonische Atmosphäre zu schaffen, die modern, schnörkellos und trotzdem gemütlich ist. Zu den Zimmern führen tiefschwarze Korridore, die nur von einem Lichtstreifen im Boden beleuchtet werden – umso größer ist die Überraschung, wenn man die luftigen und hellen Räume betritt. Minimal ausgestattet und in warmen Farben gehalten, besitzen sie Holzböden und -möbel, Ledervorhänge und Designklassiker wie Bertoias Fledermausstuhl. Von der Dachterrasse mit Pool eröffnet sich ein kinotauglicher Ausblick über La Pedrera bis zum Meer.

Connu pour ces excellents restaurants dans Barcelone, le groupe Tragaluz a cartonné avec son premier hôtel. Celui-ci est fréquenté par les gens de la mode et les Barcelonais branchés qui adorent se prélasser dans les sofas du lobby ou dans le fauteuil « Egg Chair » d'Arne Jacobsen, près de la cheminée. Les deux restaurants et le club Ommsession au sous-sol sont vite devenus, eux aussi, la Mecque des faiseurs de tendance. Les designers de l'hôtel ont réussi à créer une atmosphère harmonieuse, à la fois moderne, sobre et confortable. Pour accéder aux chambres, vous devez suivre des couloirs plongés dans les ténèbres et uniquement éclairés par une bande de lumière sur le sol. La surprise est donc d'autant plus grande quand on découvre les chambres claires et aérées. Minimalistes et peintes dans des couleurs chaudes, elles comprennent des meubles en bois, des tentures en cuir et des classiques du design comme la chaise chauve-souris de Bertoia. Depuis la terrasse et sa piscine, le client a une vue époustouflante sur « La Pedrera » et la mer au loin.

Rates: Double rooms from 375 € (single occupancy from 295 €), suites from 550 €. Breakfast 22 €.
Rooms: 59 rooms and suites.
Cuisine: The restaurant Moo-Vida serves seasonal dishes. The "Moo" of the famed Roca brothers specialises in Catalan haute cuisine and has been awarded one Michelin star.
History: Opened in December 2003.
X-Factor: The incredible massages in the Spaciomm spa.
Internet: WLAN (free of charge).

Preise: DZ ab 375 € (zur Einzelnutzung ab 295 €), Suite ab 550 €. Frühstück 22 €.
Zimmer: 59 Zimmer und Suiten.
Küche: Das Restaurant Moo-Vida serviert saisonale Gerichte, das Moo der bekannten Brüder Roca hat sich auf katalanische Haute Cuisine spezialisiert und wurde mit einem Michelin-Stern ausgezeichnet.
Geschichte: Im Dezember 2003 eröffnet.
X-Faktor: Die herrlichen Massagen im Spaciomm-Wellnessbereich.
Internet: WLAN (kostenfrei).

Prix : Chambre double à partir de 375 € (pour 1 personne à partir de 295 €), suite à partir de 550 €. Petit-déjeuner 22 €.
Chambres : 59 chambres et suites.
Restauration : Le restaurant « Moo-Vida » sert des plats de saison, le « Moo » des célèbres frères Roca s'est spécialisé dans la haute cuisine catalane et a reçu une étoile Michelin.
Histoire : Ouvert en décembre 2003.
Le « petit plus » : Les merveilleux massages prodigués dans l'espace spa Spaciomm.
Internet : WLAN (gratuit).

1

2

3

1   Museum & architecture/Museum &
    Architektur/Musée & architecture

Fundació Antoni Tàpies
Carrer d'Aragó 255
08007 Barcelona
Tel: +34 93 487 03 15
www.fundaciotapies.org
Tues–Sun 10am–8pm
Metro: L2, L3, L4 Passeig de Gràcia

This foundation, established in 1984 by the
Catalan artist Antoni Tàpies, promotes the
study and understanding of contemporary
art and culture in Barcelona. In 1990, the
museum opened its doors in the building
of a former publishing house, designed by
Lluís Domènech i Montaner, Barcelona's
most celebrated architect after Gaudí. An
airy, cloud-like wire sculpture by Tàpies
hovers over the Moorish-inspired brick
building. It is really worth a visit. Tàpies has
been one of Spain's most influential artists
since the Second World War, and the
foundation owns the most comprehensive
collection of his works. It also exhibits works
by international contemporary artists.

Die Stiftung wurde 1984 vom katalanischen Künstler Antoni Tàpies ins Leben
gerufen – mit dem Ziel, das Studium und
Verständnis zeitgenössischer Kunst und
Kultur in Barcelona zu fördern. 1990 wurden die Pforten des Museums geöffnet.
Das Gebäude war von Lluís Domènech
i Montaner, dem neben Gaudí wichtigsten
Architekten in Barcelona, 1885 für einen
Verlag gebaut worden. Über dem maurisch
inspirierten Backsteinbau schwebt eine
wolkenähnliche luftige Skulptur aus Metall-
drähten von Tàpies, eine sehenswerte
Kombination. Der Stiftung gehört die
umfangreichste Sammlung von Tàpies-
Arbeiten (er gilt als bedeutendster Künstler
Spaniens nach dem Zweiten Weltkrieg);
zudem zeigt sie Ausstellungen internationaler zeitgenössischer Künstler.

Créée en 1984 par l'artiste catalan Antoni
Tàpies, la fondation a pour vocation de
promouvoir l'étude et la connaissance de
la culture et de l'art contemporains à
Barcelone. Le musée a ouvert ses portes
en 1990. Il est installé dans un bâtiment

construit en 1885 pour une maison
d'édition par Lluís Domènech i Montaner,
l'architecte le plus important de Barcelone
avec Gaudí. Au-dessus de la construction
en brique d'inspiration mauresque flotte
comme un nuage une sculpture aérienne
en métal de Tàpies : une combinaison à
voir absolument. La fondation héberge
la plus vaste collection des œuvres de
Tàpies (considéré comme le plus grand
artiste espagnol de l'après-guerre). Elle
organise par ailleurs des expositions
d'artistes contemporains du monde entier.

---

2   Tapas bar/Tapas-Bar/Bar à tapas

Bar Mut
Pau Claris 192
08037 Barcelona
Tel: +34 93 217 43 38
Mon–Fri 8am–midnight, Sat/Sun midday
to midnight
Metro: L3, L5 Diagonal

This cosy bar is decorated like an upmarket
bodega and attracts an interesting clientele. It's the ideal place to meet friends for
a few tasty tapas and a glass of wine. The
staff is very friendly.

Diese gemütliche Bar ist im Stil einer ge-
hobenen Bodega eingerichtet und zieht
ein sympathisches Publikum an. Sie ist
ideal, um sich mit Freunden auf ein paar
leckere Tapas und ein Glas Wein zu treffen
– besonders angenehm finde ich den
freundlichen Service.

Ce bar confortable aménagé dans le style
d'une bodega haut de gamme attire un
public sympathique. Elle est parfaite pour
rencontrer des amis autour d'un verre de
vin et d'une assiette de tapas. J'ai beaucoup apprécié la gentillesse des serveurs.

---

3   Photography books & gallery/
    Fotografie-Bücher & Galerie/
    Livres de photographie & galerie

Kowasa
Carrer de Mallorca 235
08008 Barcelona
Tel: +34 93 487 61 37

www.kowasa.com
Daily 11am–2pm and 5pm–8.30pm
Metro: L3, L5 Diagonal

Opened in 1992, this shop has Europe's
biggest selection of photography books.
You'll find every category here, from architecture to travel photography, from fashion
to photojournalism. Kowasa also has a
comprehensive archive of original works
by international and Spanish photogra-
phers on exhibit and for sale.

Dieser 1992 gegründete Laden hat europaweit die größte Auswahl an Büchern zur
Fotografie aller Sparten – von Architektur
über Reise bis hin zu Mode – sowie zum
Fotojournalismus. Außerdem besitzt Kowasa
ein umfangreiches Archiv an Originalwerken
internationaler und spanischer Fotografen,
die hier auch ausgestellt und verkauft
werden.

Ce magasin fondé en 1992 est celui qui
propose en Europe le plus grand choix de
livres sur la photographie dans tous les
domaines – de l'architecture à la mode en
passant par les voyages – ainsi que sur
le photojournalisme. Possédant en outre
un fonds important de clichés originaux
réalisés par des photographes internationaux et espagnols, Kowasa les expose et
les vend dans ce magasin.

---

4   Spanish restaurant/Spanisches
    Restaurant/Restaurant espagnol

Flash Flash Tortillería
Carrer de la Granada del Penedès 25
08006 Barcelona
Tel: +34 93 237 09 90
www.flashflashtortilleria.com
Daily 1pm–1.30am
Metro: L3, L5 Diagonal

This restaurant opened in 1970 and is still
extremely stylish and popular. Their menu
offers more than 70 different varieties of
tortillas, or Spanish omelettes. The décor
is all white, with black silhouettes of the
model Karin Leiz painted on the walls.
The motifs are based on photographs by
Leopoldo Pomés, a fashion photographer
who is also the proprietor. The interior

4

5

evokes memories of Antonioni's *Blow Up* – you are instantly transported back to the 1960s.

Dieses Restaurant wurde 1970 eröffnet und ist bis heute superstylisch und beliebt. Hier gibt es mehr als 70 Sorten Tortillas, also spanische Omeletts. Das Ambiente ist ganz in Weiß gehalten, und an die Wand wurden schwarze Silhouetten des Models Karin Leiz gemalt (nach Aufnahmen des Modefotografen und Besitzers Leopoldo Pomés) – damit erinnert das Interieur an Antonionis Film „Blow up". Wie im Time-Tunnel zurück in die 1960er!

Ouvert en 1970, ce restaurant méga cool n'a rien perdu de sa popularité. La carte compte soixante-dix variétés de tortillas, l'omelette espagnole. L'intérieur est tout en blanc avec, au mur, les silhouettes noires du modèle Karin Leiz (peintes d'après les clichés de Leopoldo Pomés, photographe de mode et propriétaire du lieu) – il fait penser à « Blow up », le film d'Antonioni. Nous voilà revenus dans les années 1960 !

5   Spanish fashion/Spanische Mode/
     Mode espagnole

Josep Font

Carrer de Provença 304
08008 Barcelona
Tel: +34 93 487 21 10
www.josepfont.com
Mon–Sat 10am–8.30pm
Metro: L3, L5 Diagonal

Josep Font is one of the most interesting contemporary Spanish fashion designers. He still keeps his headquarters in Barcelona, his hometown, even though he has branches in Paris, Madrid and Bilbao. Colourfully patterned Spanish tiles pave the floor of his roomy shop in Carrer de Provença, but the rest of the décor is minimalist. His seductive creations with a romantic touch hang from bars along the right and left sides of the shop. A large wooden table that serves as a sales counter is located at the back, so your attention isn't distracted from the beautiful clothes.

Josep Font ist einer der interessantesten

spanischen Modedesigner der Gegenwart. Er hat in seiner Heimatstadt Barcelona nach wie vor seinen Hauptsitz, obwohl er auch in Paris, Madrid und Bilbao Filialen besitzt. Sein großzügiger Laden in der Carrer de Provença ist mit bunten, unterschiedlich gemusterten spanischen Fliesen ausgelegt, der Rest ist sehr minimalistisch gehalten. Rechts und links hängen an schlichten Stangen seine verführerischen, romantisch angehauchten Kreationen. Erst am Ende steht ein großer Holztisch als Verkaufstresen, sodass der Blick für die Mode frei bleibt.

Josep Font est l'un des créateurs de mode espagnols les plus intéressants de notre époque. Bien qu'il possède aussi des filiales à Paris, Madrid et Bilbao, il a gardé sa maison-mère à Barcelone, la ville où il est né. Le sol de sa boutique spacieuse sur la Carrer de Provença est recouvert d'un carrelage espagnol coloré présentant différents motifs, le reste étant très minimaliste. À droite et à gauche, ses créations affriolantes, un brin romantiques, sont tout simplement suspendues à des tringles. La grande table en bois servant à la vente est reléguée au fond afin que les vêtements restent à l'honneur.

Personal discoveries/Eigene
Entdeckungen/Découvertes personnelles :

987
Barcelona Hotel

Carrer de Mallorca, 288   08037 Barcelona
☎ +34 93 476 33 96
reservas@987barcelonahotel.com
www.987hotels.com
Metro: L2, L3, L4 Passeig de Gràcia
Booking: www.great-escapes-hotels.com

987 Barcelona Hotel

This hotel is within walking distance of the Passeig de Gràcia and Gaudí's Casa Milà. It is in a beautiful building that's typical of turn-of-the-century Barcelona, with quirky bay windows, floral stucco ceilings and spacious rooms. The designers have tried to combine the original architecture with avant-garde interiors, and in some rooms they've even kept the fancifully corniced and gilded ceilings. Classy, custom chocolate-brown furniture and modern bathrooms are colourfully accented with lime green and turquoise. Black and white prints by Catalan photographer Pep Escoda, who also took the photos for this book, adorn the walls of the rooms. The comfortable, relaxed hotel restaurant specialises in Mediterranean cuisine. If the weather is good, you can enjoy your "café con leche" on the patio.

Dieses Hotel liegt in Gehweite zum Passeig de Gràcia und damit zu Gaudís Casa Milà. Es befindet sich in einem der wunderschönen Barceloner Bauten der Jahrhundertwende mit exzentrischen Erkerchen, floralem Stuck und großzügigen Grundrissen. Die Designer haben versucht, die alte Architektur mit avantgardistischen Interieurs zu verbinden – so sind in einigen Räumen verspielte, vergoldete Stuckdecken erhalten geblieben. Schicke schokoladenbraune, maßgefertigte Möbel sowie moderne Bäder wurden kontrastreich mit limettengrünen und türkisblauen Akzenten versehen. In jedem Zimmer hängen außerdem originale Schwarz-Weiß-Aufnahmen des katalanischen Fotografen Pep Escoda, der auch für dieses Buch die Fotografien gemacht hat. Das Restaurant des Hotels hat sich auf mediterrane Küche spezialisiert und besitzt ein entspanntes Ambiente. Im Innenhof kann man bei schönem Wetter seinen „café con leche" unter freiem Himmel trinken.

Situé à quelques pas du Passeig de Gràcia et par conséquent de la Casa Milà de Gaudí, cet hôtel se trouve dans l'un des plus beaux immeubles de Barcelone construits aux alentours de 1900. Les designers ont associé à l'architecture spacieuse, avec ses encorbellements excentriques et ses stucs sculptés de fleurs, une décoration intérieure avant-gardiste. Dans certaines chambres, ils ont ainsi conservé les plafonds de stuc doré et leurs nombreux ornements. Des accents de couleur vert citron et bleu turquoise forment un joli contraste avec l'élégant mobilier marron chocolat, fabriqué sur mesure, et les salles de bains modernes. Dans chaque chambre sont accrochés au mur des clichés originaux en noir et blanc du photographe catalan Pep Escoda, lequel a également réalisé les photographies de cet ouvrage. Spécialisé dans la cuisine méditerranéenne, le restaurant de l'hôtel possède une atmosphère décontractée. Quand il fait beau, le client peut boire son « café con leche » en plein air, dans la cour intérieure.

Rates: Single rooms from 290 €, double rooms from 320 €, suites from 450 €. Breakfast 12 €.
Rooms: 93 rooms and suites.
Cuisine: The restaurant serves market-fresh Mediterranean cuisine to the accompaniment of an ingenious light and sound design.
History: Opened in April 2007.
X-Factor: The hotel aims to give its guests a complete sensory experience – and it does.
Internet: WLAN (free of charge).

Preise: EZ ab 290 €, DZ ab 320 €, Suite ab 450 €. Frühstück 12 €.
Zimmer: 93 Zimmer und Suiten.
Küche: Im Restaurant genießt man neben marktfrischer Mittelmeerküche ein raffiniertes Licht- und Sounddesign.
Geschichte: Im April 2007 eröffnet.
X-Faktor: Das Hotel möchte alle Sinne ansprechen – und das gelingt ihm auch.
Internet: WLAN (kostenfrei).

Prix : Chambre simple à partir de 290 €, chambre double à partir de 320 €, suite à partir de 450 €. Petit déjeuner 12 €.
Chambres : 93 chambres et suites.
Restauration : Dispositif raffiné de son et lumière au restaurant où l'on sert une cuisine méditerranéenne avec des produits frais achetés sur le marché.
Histoire : Ouvert en avril 2007.
Le « petit plus » : L'hôtel veut interpeller tous nos sens … et il y parvient !
Internet : WLAN (gratuit).

1

2

3

1 Architecture & concerts/Architektur & Konzerte/Architecture & concerts

Casa Milà (La Pedrera)
Passeig de Gràcia 92
08008 Barcelona
www.lapedreraeducacio.org
www.gaudiallgaudi.com
Daily 10am–8pm
Metro: L3, L5 Diagonal

Completed in 1910, Casa Milà was named after its owner, Pere Milà Camps, but its popular name is "La Pedrera" (the quarry), because of its unusual façade. It represents Gaudí's last residential project before he devoted all his energy to the Sagrada Família. Gaudí's pioneering architectural work is certainly on display in Casa Milà. Even if you personally prefer the clean straight lines of an architect like Mies van der Rohe, or the Bauhaus style, you can appreciate that this building represents a unique and harmonious artistic synthesis. It was declared a UNESCO World Heritage Site in 1984. Some apartments still have original furnishings and are open for public viewing; other apartments are rented privately. The summer concerts (Fridays and Saturdays from July to September) are fabulous; enjoy them with a cocktail on the roof terrace with its famous, fantastically shaped chimney stacks.

Die 1910 vervollständigte Casa Milà wurde nach ihrem Besitzer Pere Milà Camps benannt – im Volksmund nennt man sie wegen ihrer eigenartigen Fassade aber auch „La Pedrera" (Steinbruch). Sie war der letzte Wohnbau Gaudís, bevor er seine ganze Kraft der Sagrada Família widmete. Bei der Casa Milà leistete Gaudí in vielen Bereichen architektonische Pionierarbeit; und selbst wenn man eher auf die Geradlinigkeit eines Mies van der Rohe oder des Bauhauses steht, ist dieses Gebäude ein in sich stimmiges, einzigartiges Gesamtkunstwerk, das von der UNESCO 1984 zum Weltkulturerbe erklärt wurde. Einzelne Wohnungen sind mit Originalgegenständen eingerichtet und können besichtigt werden, andere Apartments sind nach wie vor privat vermietet. Traumhaft sind die Sommerkonzerte (Juli–September,

Fr und Sa) bei einem Cocktail auf der Dachterrasse mit ihren berühmten, fantasievoll geformten Kaminen.

Achevée en 1910, la Casa Milà a été nommée d'après son propriétaire Pere, mais elle est aussi surnommée familièrement « La Pedrera » (la carrière) en raison de sa façade totalement insolite. Elle fut la dernière construction civile de Gaudí avant qu'il ne consacre toute son énergie à la Sagrada Família. Dans la Casa Milà, Gaudí a effectué un travail de pionnier à de nombreux égards. Même si l'on est un adepte des lignes droites de Mies van der Rohe ou du Bauhaus, on ne peut s'empêcher d'admirer cette œuvre d'art totale absolument unique dans son genre et inscrite par l'UNESCO au patrimoine mondial en 1984. Quelques appartements ont encore leur décoration d'origine et peuvent être visités, les autres sont loués à des particuliers. Une expérience inoubliable est d'écouter en sirotant un cocktail l'un des concerts d'été (ven et sam de juillet à septembre) donnés sur l'attique avec ses célèbres cheminées.

2 Tea salon & more/Teesalon & more/ Salon de thé & plus

Farga
Avinguda Diagonal 391
08008 Barcelona
Tel: +34 93 416 01 12
www.fargabarcelona.com
Mon–Fri 8am–midnight, Sat 9am–11pm,
Sun 9am–11pm
Metro: L3, L5 Diagonal

This is one of those classic places I could visit at any time of day – a delightful combination of restaurant, bar and tea salon. The interior is decorated in an elegant '60s style, with shining mahogany and brass, tall cabinets and leather bar stools – I prefer to sit at the long bar. Professional waiters provide excellent service – they bring your fresh salads, sandwiches, tapas or delicious cakes in a flash.

Dies ist eines der klassischen Etablissements, die ich zu jeder Uhrzeit besuchen könnte – eine wunderbare Mischung aus

Restaurant, Bar und Teesalon. Das Interieur gibt sich im klassisch-eleganten Stil der 1960er: mit glänzendem Mahagoni und Messing, langen Vitrinen sowie lederbezogenen Barhockern (am liebsten sitze ich direkt an der langen Theke). Erfahrene Ober bieten einen exzellenten Service und bringen in Windeseile frische Salate, Sandwiches, Tapas oder köstliche Kuchen.

Merveilleux mélange de restaurant, bar et de salon de thé, voici l'un des établissements que je pourrais fréquenter à n'importe quelle heure de la journée. L'intérieur est décoré dans un style classique et élégant des années 1960 : bois d'acajou, laiton, grandes vitrines et tabourets de bar capitonés en cuir (la meilleure place pour moi est directement au comptoir). Des serveurs parfaitement stylés vous apporteront en un clin d'œil des salades, des sandwiches et des tapas succulents ou encore de délicieux gâteaux.

3 Furniture & more/Möbel & more/ Mobilier & plus

Coriumcasa
Carrer de Provença 268
08008 Barcelona
Tel: +34 93 272 12 24
www.coriumcasa.com
Mon–Sat 10am–2pm and 4.30pm–8.30pm
Metro: L3, L5 Diagonal

Since the 1992 Olympics, Barcelona has been a designer-obsessed city, and design and furniture shops are still popping up everywhere. Opened in 2002, Coriumcasa doesn't chase the trends, but instead presents a small, tasteful assortment of carefully selected furniture. You can also find distinctive and unusual teapots, bedcovers, cushions, candles and ceramics. The sister shop, Corium (Passeig de Gràcia 106), sells design and lifestyle books, plus accessories by Paul Smith, Ex voto and Mizensir.

Barcelona ist seit den Olympischen Spielen 1992 eine Stadt, in der ein Designkult herrscht – noch heute sprießen überall Design- und Möbelläden aus dem Boden. Coriumcasa wurde 2002 eröffnet, rennt

4

5

Cervecería Catalana is the oldest tapas bar in Barcelona and has always been very popular with the locals. Numerous tapas and "montaditos" (little sandwiches) are displayed in two tall glass cabinets, one on each side of the entrance. This is a busy place; guests waiting for a rare empty table should order a "cava" at one of the two bars, and enjoy a couple of tapas before the meal.

Die Cervecería Catalana ist die älteste Tapas-Bar in Barcelona – das große Lokal ist bis heute bei den Einheimischen sehr beliebt. Hinter zwei langen Vitrinen rechts und links des Eingangs werden ungezählte Tapas und „montaditos" (kleine belegte Brote) präsentiert. Gäste, die auf einen der begehrten Tische warten müssen, trinken am besten an einer der beiden Theken solange einen „cava" und naschen schon mal von den Tapas.

La Cervecería Catalana est le plus ancien bar à tapas de Barcelone et a gardé toute sa popularité auprès des habitants de la ville. D'innombrables tapas et « montaditos » (mini-sandwichs) sont présentés en vitrine à droite et à gauche de l'entrée. En attendant qu'une table soit libre, les clients sont assis à l'un des deux comptoirs et en profitent pour boire un « cava » et grignoter quelques tapas.

Personal discoveries/Eigene Entdeckungen/Découvertes personnelles :

_____

_____

_____

_____

_____

_____

_____

_____

_____

_____

_____

_____

_____

_____

_____

aber nicht dem aktuellsten Trend hinterher, sondern präsentiert eine kleine, feine Auswahl an ausgesuchten Möbeln. Zudem findet man hier besondere Teekannen, Plaids, Kissen, Kerzen und Keramik. Im Schwesterladen Corium (Passeig de Gràcia 106) gibt es Bücher zum Thema Design und Lifestyle sowie Accessoires von Marken wie Paul Smith, Ex voto oder Mizensir.

Depuis les Jeux olympiques de 1992, Barcelone est une ville où domine le culte du design. Aujourd'hui encore les magasins de meubles et de design s'implantent un peu partout. Ouvert en 2002, Coriumcasa ne court pas derrière les tendances en vogue, mais présente un petit éventail de meubles sélectionnés avec soin. Vous y trouverez aussi des cafetières, des plaids, des coussins, des bougies et des céramiques particulièrement originaux. La boutique jumelle Corium (Passeig de Gràcia 106) propose des livres sur les thèmes du design et du lifestyle ainsi que des accessoires de marques comme Paul Smith, Ex voto ou Mizensir.

4   Legendary design shop/Legendärer Designshop/Designshop légendaire

Vinçon
Passeig de Gràcia 96
08008 Barcelona
Tel: +34 93 215 60 50
www.vincon.com
Mon–Sat 10am–8.30pm
Metro: L3, L5 Diagonal

Barcelona's legendary and oldest design shop has occupied this 19th-century building since 1941. Furniture, lamps, bathroom accessories, kitchen utensils, garden furniture and office items by international and Spanish designers are on display over three floors. There are more than 10,000 products in their catalogue, most of which can be viewed and ordered online. The furniture showroom on the first floor is an absolute must-see. The tall rooms with original wood panelling and a huge fireplace make an exquisite setting for the furniture. This very stately floor used to belong to the "Modernisme" painter Ramon

Casas in 1900. My tip: take a trip to the roof garden, for a view of La Pedrera.

Das erste und legendärste aller Designgeschäfte in Barcelona befindet sich seit 1941 in diesem historischen Gebäude von 1899. Auf drei Etagen werden hier Möbel, Lampen, Bad- und Küchenutensilien, Gartenmöbel sowie Büro-Accessoires von internationalen und auch spanischen Designern präsentiert. Das Programm umfasst mehr als 10.000 Produkte – man kann heute die Stücke sogar fast alle online anschauen und bestellen. Im ersten Geschoss gibt es einen Showroom für Möbel, den man unbedingt besuchen sollte – die hohen und original holzvertäfelten Räume mit riesigem Kamin sind eine fantastische Kulisse (diese hochherrschaftliche Etage gehörte 1900 dem modernistischen Maler Ramon Casas). Ich empfehle zudem einen Abstecher auf den Dachgarten mit Ausblick auf La Pedrera.

Le premier et le plus légendaire de tous les magasins design de Barcelone se trouve depuis 1941 dans cet immeuble historique datant de 1899. Meubles, lampes, ustensiles sanitaires et de cuisine, mobilier de jardin et accessoires de bureau, dessinés par des designers espagnols et internationaux, sont présentés ici sur trois étages. Le magasin propose plus de dix mille produits dont la quasi-totalité peut être commandée sur Internet. On ne manquera pas de visiter le showroom des meubles au premier étage. Les salles à haut plafond et aux boiseries d'origine constituent avec leur énorme cheminée un décor fantastique (cet étage aux allures majestueuses a appartenu en 1900 au peintre moderniste Ramon Casas). Je vous recommande aussi de faire un détour sur le toit-jardin avec sa vue sur « La Pedrera ».

5   Cervecería/Cervecería/Cervecería

Cervecería Catalana
Carrer de Mallorca 236
08007 Barcelona
Tel: +34 93 216 03 68
Daily 1pm–1am
Metro: L2, L3, L4 Passeig de Gràcia

Gràcia/
L'Eixample

170 Hotel Casa Fuster
180 Hostal Palacios

1 Modernist architecture/Modernistische Architektur/
Architecture moderniste
Centre del Modernisme

2 Japanese restaurant/Japanisches Restaurant/
Restaurant japonais
El Japonés

3 Spanish shoes/Spanische Schuhe/Chaussures espagnoles
Muxart

4 Glamorous restaurant/Glamouröses Restaurant/
Restaurant glamour
Noti

5 Spanish leather goods/Spanische Lederwaren/
Maroquinerie espagnole
Loewe

---

1 Fashion/Mode/Mode
Jean Pierre Bua

2 Bar/Bar/Bar
Dry Martini

3 Spanish shoes/Spanische Schuhe/Chaussures espagnoles
Camper

4 Cervecería/Cervecería/Cervecería
Cervecería Ciudad Condal

5 Fashion/Designermode/Mode
Jean Pierre Symbol

Hotel
Casa Fuster

Passeig de Gràcia, 132   08008 Barcelona
☎ +34 93 255 30 00   +34 93 255 30 02
info@hotelcasafuster.com
www.hotelcasafuster.com
Metro: L3, L5 Diagonal
Booking: www.great-escapes-hotels.com

Hotel Casa Fuster

Too little has been done for one, too much for the other. The Hotel España (see p. 60) and the Casa Fuster were both designed by Lluís Domènech i Montaner and are now hotels. The former, still awaiting renovation, is a staple of package tours; the latter has been transformed into an expensive, five-star hotel. The Casa Fuster was considered one of the most beautiful buildings in the city at the beginning of the 20th century. The magnificent architecture is best seen and admired from ground level, where the coaches used to stop and where the reception is located today. Another good vantage point is in Café Vienés, the former salon. Marvel at the fantastically decorated pillars and ceilings, a unique Art Nouveau feature. The rooms are all decorated in subdued natural shades, which, unfortunately, have a rather depressing effect. And the tacky oscillating taffeta and iridescent velvet fabrics are not exactly elegant or noble.

Was beim einen zu wenig, ist beim anderen zu viel geschehen: Die beiden von Lluís Domènech i Montaner erbauten Gebäude, die heute in Barcelona als Hotel dienen, sind das Hotel España (siehe Seite 60) und die Casa Fuster. Ersteres wurde bisher noch nicht renoviert und dient heute den Pauschaltouristen, Letzteres wurde in ein teures 5-Sterne-Hotel verwandelt. Anfang des 20. Jahrhunderts galt die Casa Fuster als das schönste Haus der Stadt. Die grandiose Architektur lässt sich heute vor allem in dem ebenerdigen Bereich bestaunen, dort wo einst die Kutschen hielten und heute sich die Rezeption befindet, und im Café Vienés, dem damaligen Salon. Hier kann man die fantasievoll verzierten Säulen und Decken bewundern, eine einzigartige Ausprägung des Jugendstils. Die Zimmer sind alle in müden Naturtönen gehalten, die leider etwas Depressives haben; und auch die Materialien, wie oszillierender Taft und changierender Samt, wirken nicht unbedingt edel oder elegant.

Ce qui manque à l'un est en abondance chez l'autre : les deux édifices construits par Lluís Domènech i Montaner, qui servent aujourd'hui d'hôtels à Barcelone, sont l'España (voir page 60) et la Casa Fuster. Le premier n'a pas encore été rénové et accueille les voyageurs à forfait, le second a été transformé en un coûteux hôtel 5 étoiles. Au début du XXe siècle, la Casa Fuster était considérée comme la plus belle maison de la ville. Aujourd'hui, on peut surtout contempler son architecture grandiose dans l'espace au niveau du sol, là où jadis les fiacres s'arrêtaient et où se trouve maintenant la réception, ainsi qu'au « Café Vienés », l'ancien salon. Là, on admirera les colonnes et les plafonds ornés avec beaucoup d'imagination dans un style art nouveau très original. Les chambres sont toutes décorées dans des tons naturels un peu fatigués qui leur confèrent malheureusement un air tristounet. Le choix des étoffes comme le taffetas et le satin à l'aspect changeant ne donne pas vraiment non plus une impression de luxe ou d'élégance.

Rates: Single and double rooms from 420 €, suites from 620 €. Breakfast 25 €.
Rooms: 96 rooms and suites.
Cuisine: Tea and coffee is served in Café Vienés. The restaurant Galaxó offers a Mediterranean menu.
History: Originally built for Mariano Fuster in 1908–11.
X-Factor: The roof terrace with a swimming pool boasts a breathtaking view of the city and the sea.
Internet: WLAN (in Café Vienés free of charge), and broadband (free of charge in the rooms).

Preise: EZ/DZ ab 420 €, Suite ab 620 €. Frühstück 25 €.
Zimmer: 96 Zimmer und Suiten.
Küche: Im Café Vienés werden Tee und Kaffee serviert. Das Restaurant Galaxó hat eine mediterrane Karte.
Geschichte: Ursprünglich von 1908–1911 für Mariano Fuster erbaut.
X-Faktor: Die Dachterrasse mit Pool bietet einen traumhaften Blick über die Stadt und das Meer.
Internet: WLAN (kostenfrei, im Café Vienés), Breitband (kostenfrei, in den Zimmern).

Prix : Chambre simple ou double à partir de 420 €, suite à partir de 620 €. Petit déjeuner 25 €.
Chambres : 96 chambres et suites.
Restauration : Thé et café au « Café Vienés », carte méditerranéenne au restaurant « Galaxó ».
Histoire : Au départ, construit de 1908 à 1911 pour Mariano Fuster.
Le « petit plus » : Le toit-terrasse avec sa piscine offre une vue magnifique sur la ville et la mer.
Internet : WLAN (gratuit au « Café Vienés »), haut débit (gratuit dans les chambres).

1   2   3

1   Modernist architecture/
     Modernistische Architektur/
     Architecture moderniste

Centre del Modernisme

Hospital de la Santa Creu i Sant Pau
Carrer de Sant Antoni Maria Claret 167
08025 Barcelona
Tel: +34 93 207 66 21
www.santpau.es
Daily 10am–2pm. Guided tours: 10.15am
and 12.15pm in English, 11.15am in
Catalan, 1.15pm in Spanish.
Metro: L5 Hospital de Sant Pau

Catalan banker Pau Gil commissioned the
building of a hospital in his will. The architect Lluís Domènech i Montaner began
constructing the Hospital de la Santa Creu
i Sant Pau with Gil's resources in 1902.
He planned 48 separate pavilions for the
individual medical departments in a park-
like garden. The connecting passages,
like the technical equipment, were built
underground. After the death of Lluís
Domènech in 1923, the work was continued
by his son and completed seven years later.
The hospital is still used as a clinic today,
although it has been declared a UNESCO
World Heritage Site along with Domènech's
Palau de la Música Catalana (see p. 123).

Der katalanische Bankier Pau Gil verfügte
in seinem Testament den Bau eines
Krankenhauses. Mit Gils Mitteln begann
der Architekt Lluís Domènech i Montaner
1902, das Hospital de la Santa Creu i Sant
Pau zu errichten. Er plante 48 voneinander
unabhängige Pavillons für die verschiedenen
medizinischen Abteilungen in einer weit-
läufigen Gartenanlage. Die Verbindungs-
gänge sind, wie alle anderen technischen
Einrichtungen, unter die Erde verlegt.
Der Bau wurde nach dem Tod von Lluís
Domènech 1923 von seinem Sohn weiter-
geführt und sieben Jahre später beendet.
Noch heute wird das Hospital als Klinik
genutzt, dabei steht es zusammen mit
Domènechs Palau de la Música Catalana
(siehe Seite 123) auf der UNESCO-Liste
der Weltkulturerbe.

Dans son testament, le banquier catalan
Pau Gil spécifia qu'une partie de ses biens
devait être employée à la construction d'un
hôpital baptisé plus tard Hospital de la
Santa Creu i Sant Pau. Ce fut l'architecte
Lluís Domènech i Montaner qui, en 1902,
en dessina les plans. Il avait prévu quarante-
huit pavillons disséminés dans un vaste
parc. Les communications entre les pavillons,
tout comme les autres installations techniques, sont souterraines. Après la mort de
Lluís Domènech en 1923, son fils reprit la
direction des travaux qui furent achevés
sept ans plus tard. L'hôpital est encore en
service de nos jours et figure avec le Palau
de la Música Catalana de Domènech (voir
page 123) sur la liste du patrimoine mondial de l'UNESCO.

2   Japanese restaurant/Japanisches
     Restaurant/Restaurant japonais

El Japonés

Passatge de la Concepció 2
08008 Barcelona
Tel: +34 93 487 25 92
www.eljaponesdeltragaluz.com
Lunch daily 1.30pm–4pm. Dinner Sun–Wed
8.30pm–midnight, Thurs 8pm–0.30am,
Fri/Sat 8pm–1am.
Metro: L3, L5 Diagonal

If you need a change from oily Spanish
food, then El Japonés is just the place for
you. The restaurant is situated in a romantic pedestrian side street and attracts a
young and varied clientele with Asian
cuisine ranging from tempura to sushi. You
are served at long wooden tables and
benches in a Japanese-minimalist ambience,
which is nevertheless still very laid back.
Delicious food, and a pleasant atmosphere.

Wer Abwechslung vom fetten spanischen
Essen braucht, ist bei El Japonés genau
richtig. Das Restaurant liegt in einer
romantischen, autofreien Passage und
lockt mit seiner asiatischen Küche von
Tempura bis Sushi ein junges, gemischtes
Publikum an. Serviert wird in einem japa-
nisch-minimalistischen und trotzdem
gemütlichen Ambiente mit langen Holz-
tischen und -bänken. Sehr lecker und
sehr nette Atmosphäre.

« El Japonés » est parfait si vous êtes un

peu las de la nourriture espagnole somme
toute assez grasse. Situé dans une rue
piétonne romantique, le restaurant attire
avec sa cuisine asiatique et ses sushis un
public jeune et hétéroclite. L'ambiance est
minimaliste et quand même confortable
avec de grandes tables et des bancs en
bois. Très bon et très sympa.

3   Spanish shoes/Spanische Schuhe/
     Chaussures espagnoles

Muxart

Carrer del Rosselló 230
08008 Barcelona
Tel: +34 93 488 10 64
www.muxart.com
Mon–Sat 10am–2pm and 4.30pm–8.30pm
Metro: L3, L5 Diagonal

Everyone knows that jeans and a T-shirt can
be really chic as long as you're wearing the
right shoes. The Catalan Hermenegildo
Muxart knows his customers' taste and
has very successfully established the
company Muxart, where Barcelona's
fashion-savvy head when they're looking
for fancy shoes.

Es ist bekannt, dass man in Jeans und
T-Shirt superchic ist, wenn man die richtigen
Schuhe dazu trägt. Und der Katalane
Hermenegildo Muxart weiß, was seine
Kundinnen wünschen und hat mit viel
Erfolg die Firma Muxart gegründet, bei
der die trendbewusste Barceloneserin
gerne ein paar der meist ausgefallenen
Modelle ersteht.

Tout le monde sait qu'on peut être chic en
jeans et t-shirt, tout dépend de la chaussure
qu'on porte. Et le catalan Hermenegildo
Muxart sait ce que veulent ses clientes. Il
a créé avec succès la firme « Muxart », où
la Barcelonaise tendance achète volontiers
l'un de ses modèles extravagants.

4   Glamorous restaurant/Glamouröses
     Restaurant/Restaurant glamour

Noti

Carrer de Roger de Llúria 35–37
08009 Barcelona

4

5

Tel: +34 93 342 66 73
www.noti-universal.com
Mon–Fri 1.30pm–4pm and 8.30pm–
midnight, Sat/Sun 8.30pm–midnight.
Bar open until 2.30am.
Metro: L2, L3, L4 Passeig de Gràcia

The most glamorous restaurant in Barcelona
is housed in the former headquarters of
the newspaper "El Noticiero Universal".
The building was awarded the important
FAD Architecture Prize in 1965. Francesc
Pons designed the restaurant's smart
interior (the black, white, red and gold
décor was inspired by the "toreo", the
bullfight). The creative and the beautiful
stage their glamorous entrances before
this backdrop – this is the place to see
and be seen. The menu is small but select.
If you only want a drink, then order a "cava"
or a cocktail at the smart GoodBar, a
pleasure in itself.

Im ehemaligen Hauptsitz der Zeitung El
Noticiero Universal (das Gebäude gewann
1965 den wichtigen FAD-Architekturpreis)
befindet sich das glamouröseste Restaurant Barcelonas. Das elegante Interieur in
Schwarz, Weiß, Rot und Gold wurde vom
Stierkampf inspiriert und von Francesc
Pons gestaltet. Vor dieser Kulisse insze-
nieren die Kreativen und Schönen ihren
glamourösen Auftritt. Ein guter Ort, um zu
sehen und gesehen zu werden. Das Menü
ist kurz, aber ausgezeichnet. Wer lieber
nur einen Drink nehmen möchte, kann
einen „cava" oder Cocktail an der schicken
GoodBar bestellen, das ist schon schön
genug.

L'ancien siège du journal « El Noticiero
Universal » (le bâtiment remporta en
1965 l'important prix d'architecture FAD)
abrite le restaurant le plus glamour de
Barcelone. S'inspirant de la corrida,
Francesc Pons a aménagé l'élégant
intérieur en noir, blanc, rouge et or. C'est
dans ce décor que les artistes et les belles filles font une apparition remarquée.
Ici c'est un lieu pour voir et être vu. La
carte est succincte mais excellente. Si
vous ne désirez prendre qu'un verre, vous
pourrez commander un « cava » ou un
cocktail au très chic GoodBar et vous
serez déjà comblé !

5   Spanish leather goods/Spanische
     Lederwaren/Maroquinerie espagnole

Loewe
Passeig de Gràcia 35
08007 Barcelona
Tel: +34 93 216 04 00
www.loewe.es
Mon–Sat 10am–8.30pm
Metro: L2, L3, L4 Passeig de Gràcia

Loewe stands for luxury in Spain – it's
the equivalent of Hermès in France. Back
in 1846, Enrique Loewe set up a small
business in Madrid to sell the very best
leather accessories. His patrons have
include everyone from the King of Spain,
to celebrities like Ava Gardner, Ernest
Hemingway and Cary Grant. From 1997,
the designer Narciso Rodriguez created
the ready-to-wear collection, and José
Enrique Oña Selfa has been designing for
Loewe since 2001. His bags and fashion
are a fascinating mixture of bourgeois
luxury and sexy glamour. On top of that,
the boutique in Passeig de Gràcia has
its premises in a splendid Catalan "Modernisme" building.

Loewe ist ein Symbol für Luxus in Spanien,
so wie Hermès in Frankreich. Bereits 1846
gründete Enrique Loewe ein kleines
Geschäft in Madrid, in dem er allerfeinste
Lederaccessoires verkaufte. Der König
von Spanien und Prominente wie Ava
Gardner, Ernest Hemingway oder Cary
Grant waren hier schon Kunden. Ab 1997
kreierte der Designer Narciso Rodriguez
die Prêt-à-porter-Linie, seit 2001 ist José
Enrique Oña Selfa als Designer für Loewe
tätig. Seine Taschen und Mode sind eine
spannende Mischung aus bourgeoisem
Luxus und sexy Glamour. Die Boutique
auf dem Passeig de Gràcia ist zudem in
einem prachtvollen Bau des katalanischen
Modernismo untergebracht.

Loewe est un symbole du luxe en Espagne,
comme Hermès en France. Dès 1846,
Enrique Loewe fonda un petit commerce
à Madrid proposant de la maroquinerie de
luxe. Plus tard, le roi d'Espagne et de nombreuses célébrités comme Ava Gardner,
Ernest Hemingway ou Cary Grant firent

partie de la clientèle. À partir de 1997 le
styliste Narciso Rodriguez créa la ligne
de prêt-à-porter, et depuis 2001 c'est
José Enrique Oña Selfa qui se charge des
créations pour Loewe. Ses sacs et vêtements sont un mélange excitant de luxe
bourgeois et de glamour sexy. De plus, la
boutique sur le Passeig de Gràcia se
trouve dans un sompteux bâtiment du
« modernismo » catalan.

Personal discoveries/Eigene
Entdeckungen/Découvertes personnelles :

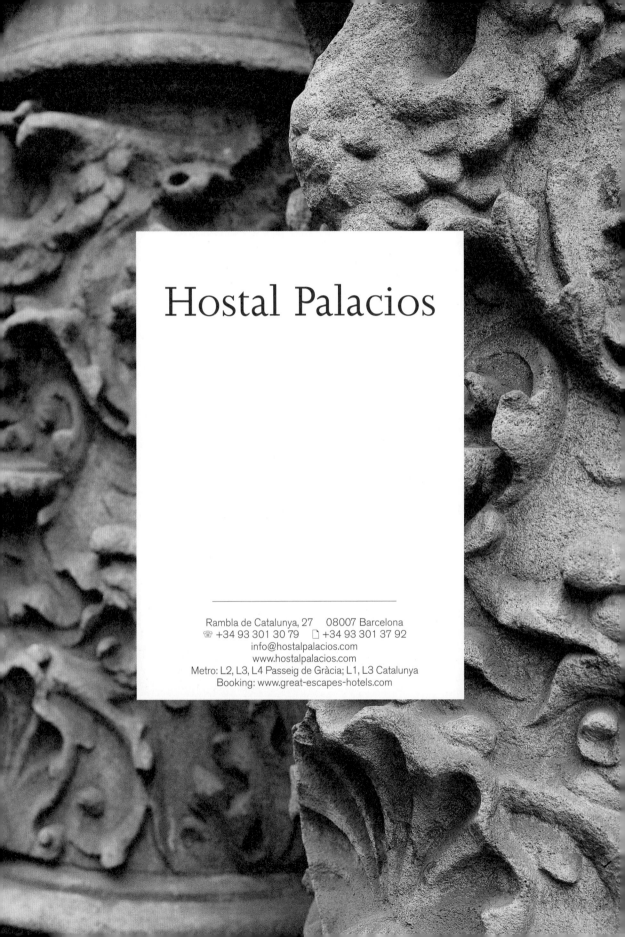

Hostal Palacios

Rambla de Catalunya, 27   08007 Barcelona
☎ +34 93 301 30 79   📠 +34 93 301 37 92
info@hostalpalacios.com
www.hostalpalacios.com
Metro: L2, L3, L4 Passeig de Gràcia; L1, L3 Catalunya
Booking: www.great-escapes-hotels.com

Hostal Palacios

This "hostal", housed in a listed Art Nouveau building, has an ideal location, on La Rambla de Catalunya, right in the middle of Eixample, the centre of Barcelona. It's only a short walk to sights like Gaudí's Casa Batlló and Casa Milà, and the smart shopping boulevard Passeig de Gràcia. The façade is what impresses you first, and then you step through the very stately entrance and up an imposing staircase. It leads to the first floor to the guest house – a high-ceilinged apartment that looks like it might have housed a well-to-do, turn-of-the-century Spanish family. There are only 11 rooms. The ones facing the street are really large with beautiful ceiling mouldings, bay windows and those beautiful Spanish tile floors. The traditional middle-class elegance of its past is still here on display – the striped wallpaper, the gathered curtains and wooden furniture. If only they would remove the artificial flowers and some of the dust-collectors!

Dieses Gästehaus befindet sich in einem denkmalgeschützten Jugend-stil-Gebäude in bester Lage – an der Rambla de Catalunya und mitten im Eixample, dem Zentrum Barcelonas. Von hier aus sind es nur ein paar Schritte zu Sehenswürdigkeiten wie den Gaudí-Bauten Casa Batlló und Casa Milà oder den eleganten Geschäften am Passeig de Gràcia. Das Hostal Palacios besitzt bereits eine beeindruckende Fassade, dann betritt man durch ein hochherrschaftliches Entree ein imposantes Treppenhaus, das in den ersten Stock zur Pension führt, die in einer großbürgerlichen Wohnung mit hohen Decken untergebracht ist. Sie umfasst insgesamt nur elf Zimmer, wobei die Räume zur Straße hin besonders groß, mit herrlichen Stuckdecken und Erkern sowie wunderschönen spanischen Fliesenböden ausgestattet sind. Die Interieurs sind alle im traditionell bürgerlichen Stil gehalten – mit Streifentapeten, gerafften Vorhängen und Holzmöbeln. Schön wäre es nur, wenn die vielen künstlichen Stoffblumen und ein paar der vielen Staubfänger entfernt würden.

Située dans un édifice classé, de style art nouveau, cette pension bénéficie d'une situation idéale près de La Rambla de Catalunya, en plein cœur de L'Eixample, le centre de Barcelone. Elle se trouve à quelques pas des curiosités, comme la Casa Batlló et la Casa Milà de Gaudí, et des boutiques élégantes du Passeig de Gràcia. L'Hostal Palacios possède une façade impressionnante, une entrée majestueuse ainsi qu'un escalier imposant qui vous conduit au premier étage dans un appartement bourgeois aux plafonds élevés. L'hôtel ne compte que onze chambres au total. Celles donnant sur la rue sont particulièrement spacieuses et sont décorées de magnifiques plafonds en stuc, d'encorbellements et d'un sol carrelé typiquement espagnol. Les chambres sont aménagées dans un style bourgeois traditionnel avec tapisserie à rayures, draperies et meubles en bois. Ce serait encore mieux si on avait l'idée d'enlever les nombreuses fleurs artificielles et quelques-uns des attrape-poussière.

Rates: Single rooms from 55 €, double rooms from 81 €. Some rooms can be made up for 3 or 4 people. Breakfast 4.50 €.
Rooms: 11 rooms.
Cuisine: There is no "hostal" restaurant for lunch or dinner.
History: Opened in November 2001.
X-Factor: One of the few guest houses with a breakfast service! You can eat in the comfort of your room, or in the small lounge.
Internet: A PC is available, which is free of charge, and you can buy prepaid WLAN cards.

Preise: EZ ab 55 €, DZ ab 81 €. Einige Räume können auch für 3 und 4 Personen ausgestattet werden. Frühstück 4,50 €.
Zimmer: 11 Zimmer.
Küche: Das Hostal besitzt kein Restaurant für Lunch oder Dinner.
Geschichte: Im November 2001 eröffnet.
X-Faktor: Eines der wenigen Hostals mit Frühstücksservice! Man isst gemütlich im Zimmer oder in kleinen Lounges.
Internet: Ein Computer steht kostenfrei zur Verfügung, zudem kann man WLAN-Prepaid Cards kaufen.

Prix : Chambre simple à partir de 55 €, chambre double à partir de 81 €. Quelques chambres peuvent accueillir trois ou quatre personnes. Petit déjeuner 4,50 €.
Chambres : 11 chambres.
Restauration : Pas de restaurant pour le déjeuner ou le dîner.
Histoire : Ouvert en novembre 2001.
Le « petit plus » : L'un des rares Hostals avec service de petit déjeuner ! On le prend confortablement dans sa chambre ou dans de petites lounges.
Internet : Ordinateur gratuit à la disposition du client, possibilité d'acheter des cartes WLAN.

1

2

3

1   Fashion/Mode/Mode

Jean Pierre Bua
Avinguda Diagonal 469
08036 Barcelona
Tel: +34 93 439 71 00
www.jeanpierrebua.com
Mon–Sat 10am–2pm and
4.30pm–8.30pm
Metro: L5 Hospital Clínic

For over 20 years, Jean Pierre Bua, the
French expat designer, has been selling
high-quality fashion in this shop, which
was expanded and refurbished in 2003.
You can find top items for men and women
from such labels as Alexander McQueen,
John Galliano, Matthew Williamson, Dries
van Noten and Miu Miu. The boutique
resembles an atelier, and makes clever
use of mirrors.

Der Exil-Franzose Jean Pierre Bua verkauft in diesem 2003 vergrößerten und
renovierten Laden seit mehr als 20 Jahren
Mode auf höchstem Niveau. In der atelier-
ähnlichen und raffiniert mit Spiegeln
ausgestatteten Boutique gibt es die besten
Stücke von Labeln wie Alexander McQueen,
John Galliano, Matthew Williamson, Dries
van Noten und Miu Miu – für Damen und
Herren.

Depuis plus de vingt ans, le Français en
exil Jean Pierre Bua vend des vêtements
de mode de haut niveau dans cette boutique rénovée et agrandie en 2003. Dans
une ambiance d'atelier et un décor de
glaces raffiné, vous trouverez les plus
belles pièces pour hommes et femmes
de marques comme Alexander McQueen,
John Galliano, Matthew Williamson, Dries
van Noten et Miu Miu.

2   Bar/Bar/Bar

Dry Martini
Carrer d'Aribau 162-166
08036 Barcelona
Tel: +34 93 217 50 72
www.drymartinibcn.com
Sun–Thurs 1pm–2.30am, Fri/Sat 1pm–3am
Metro: L3, L5 Diagonal

A cult place for the really serious cocktail
drinker. You can choose from more than
80 varieties of gin for 007's legendary
drink. The best concoctions in town are
served at a wonderful, long wooden bar or
in elegant red banquettes. A *must*!

Ein Kult-Etablissement in Barcelona für
den wirklich wahren Cocktail-Liebhaber.
Für den legendären Lieblingsdrink von 007
kann man hier aus mehr als 80 Sorten
Gin wählen. Serviert werden die besten
Kompositionen der Stadt an einer langen,
wunderbaren Theke aus Holz oder in eleganten roten Sitzecken – ein *must*.

Un établissement culte à Barcelone pour
ceux qui aiment les cocktails. Si vous
commandez la boisson préférée de 007,
vous pourrez choisir entre quatre-vingts
variétés de gin. Pour goûter aux meilleurs
mélanges de la ville, asseyez-vous au
magnifique comptoir en bois ou sur les
élégantes banquettes rouges – un *must*.

3   Spanish shoes/Spanische Schuhe/
     Chaussures espagnoles

Camper
Carrer de Muntaner 248
08021 Barcelona
Tel: +34 93 201 31 88
www.camper.es
Mon–Sat 10am–2pm and 4pm–8pm
Metro: L5 Hospital Clínic; L3, L5 Diagonal

120 years ago, Antonio Fluxà founded a
shoe factory on Mallorca. His grandson
Lorenzo Fluxà designed the world-famous
Camper shoe in 1975. The shoe's design
reflects an ecologically aware lifestyle that
combines freedom, comfort and creativity.
The first Camper shoe store opened in
1981, here in Carrer de Muntaner. Seven
more have opened in Barcelona alone.
Because of Camper's great success (and
because the shoes really are comfortable),
there are now Camper Stores all over the
world.

Vor 120 Jahren gründete Antonio Fluxà
auf Mallorca eine Schuhfabrik. Doch den
eigentlichen Camper-Schuh entwarf sein
Enkel Lorenzo Fluxà 1975 – der einen

ökofreundlichen Lifestyle, Freiheit, Komfort und Kreativität widerspiegeln sollte.
1981 eröffnete schließlich der erste
Camper-Schuhladen hier in der Carrer
de Muntaner – sieben weitere folgten
alleine in Barcelona. Aufgrund des großen
Erfolges (und weil die Schuhe wirklich
bequem sind!) gibt es inzwischen auf der
ganzen Welt Camper-Stores.

Il y a 120 ans, Antonio Fluxà fondait son
usine de chaussures à Majorque. Mais c'est
son petit-fils Lorenzo Fluxà qui dessina en
1975 la véritable chaussure Camper avec
laquelle on associe amour de la nature,
liberté, confort et créativité. En 1981, le
premier magasin Camper ouvrit finalement
ses portes sur la Carrer de Muntaner – sept
autres allaient suivre rien qu'à Barcelone.
En raison de leur succès (et parce que ces
chaussures sont réellement confortables),
il y a maintenant des Camper-Stores
partout dans le monde.

4   Cervecería/Cervecería/Cervecería

Cervecería Ciudad Condal
Rambla de Catalunya 18
08007 Barcelona
Tel: +34 93 318 19 97
Mon–Fri 7am–1.30am,
Sat/Sun 9am–1.30am
Metro: L2, L3, L4 Passeig de Gràcia

Many different customers patronise this
place because of the incredibly large
selection of fresh tapas, "montaditos" (little
sandwiches), regional and international
sorts of beer and the friendly atmosphere.
It is always busy, and is the perfect place
to drop into for a shopping break, or after
the cinema.

Eine unglaublich große Auswahl an frischen
Tapas, „montaditos" (kleine belegte Brote),
nationale sowie internationale Biersorten
und eine freundliche Atmosphäre ziehen
ein gemischtes Publikum an. Dieses Lokal
ist immer gut besucht und perfekt, um
beim Shoppen oder nach dem Kinobesuch
eine Erfrischungspause einzulegen.

Un choix incroyable de tapas, de « montaditos » (mini-sandwichs), des marques de

4

5

bière nationales et internationales ainsi que l'atmosphère conviviale attirent un public hétéroclite. Cet établissement est toujours bien fréquenté et convient parfaitement pour se requinquer après le shopping ou une séance de cinéma.

5   Fashion/Designermode/Mode

Jean Pierre Symbol
Avinguda Diagonal 467
08036 Barcelona
Tel: +34 93 444 49 62
www.jeanpierresymbol.com
Mon–Sat 10am–2pm and
4.30pm–8.30pm
Metro: L3, L5; Diagonal

Jean Pierre Bua has opened this stylish little boutique right next to his flagship store. All his favourite labels are on show, with one small difference – the items have been taken from the casual lines of the international designers and are not as expensive as the haute-couture articles next door. Looking for something more sporty? You'll find it here, as the range also includes such brands as Lacoste.

Gleich neben seinem „Original Store" hat Jean Pierre Bua diese stylische neue Boutique eröffnet. Auch hier findet man seine Lieblingslabel – mit dem Unterschied, dass die Stücke aus den Casual-Linien der internationalen Designer stammen und preiswerter sind als die Haute-Couture-Entwürfe nebenan. Wer sportliche Mode sucht, wird ebenfalls fündig – das Portfolio umfasst Marken wie Lacoste.

Jean Pierre Bua a ouvert cette boutique inédite juste à côté de son "Original Store". On y trouve aussi ses marques préférées, mais ici on offre la ligne casual des designers internationaux, meilleur marché que les produits Haute Couture vendus à côté. Les amateurs de mode sportive ne sont pas oubliés – le portfolio comporte des marques comme Lacoste par exemple.

Personal discoveries/Eigene
Entdeckungen/Découvertes personnelles :

Montjuïc

194 AC Miramar

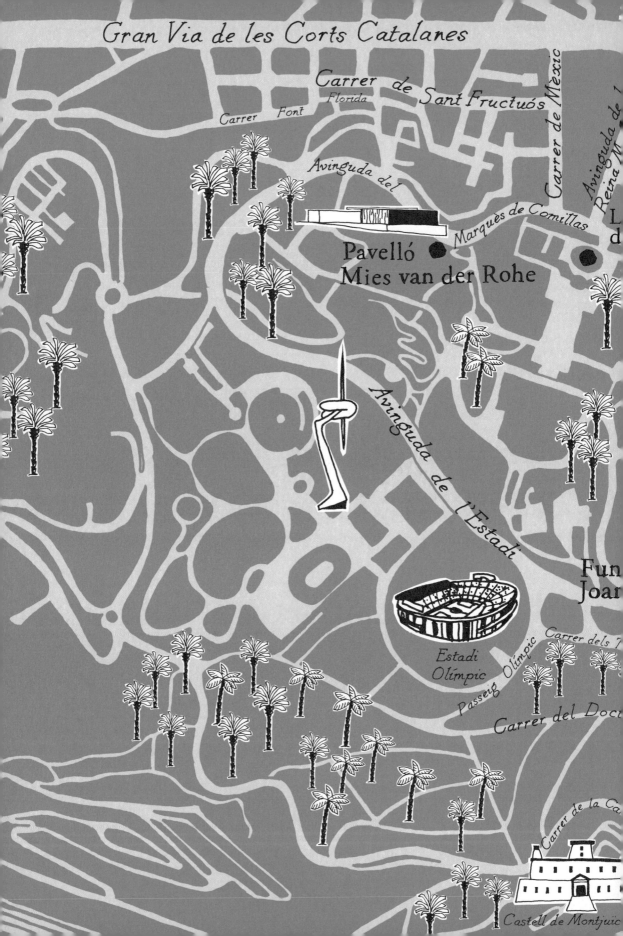

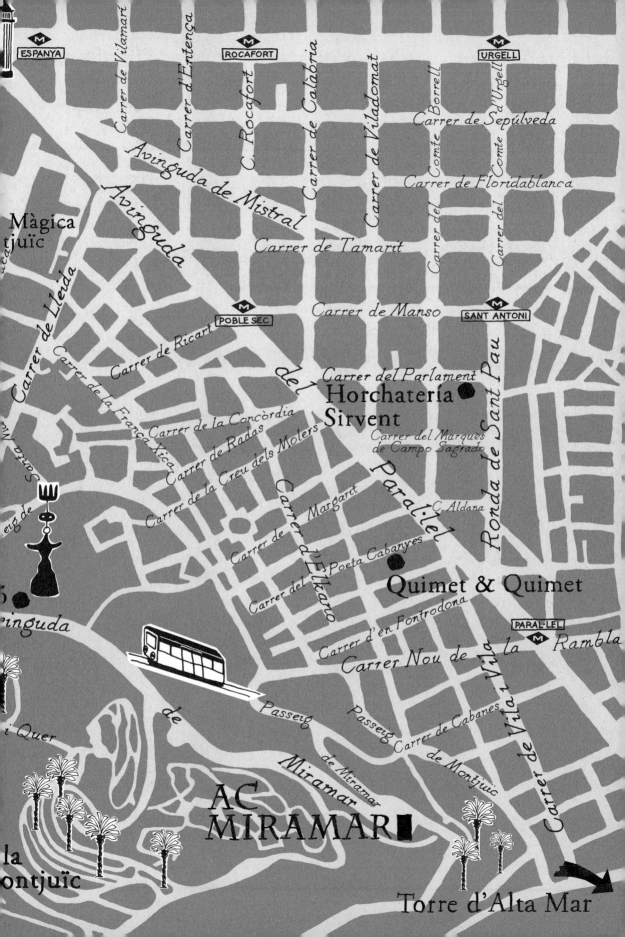

AC Miramar

Plaça de Carlos Ibáñez, 3   08038 Barcelona
☎ +34 93 281 16 00   📄 +34 93 281 16 01
acmiramar@ac-hotels.com
www.ac-hotels.com
Metro: L2, L3 Paral·lel
Booking: www.great-escapes-hotels.com

AC Miramar

Hotel Miramar, designed by the renowned Spanish architect Oscar Tusquets, is situated on Montjuïc hill, close to the centre of town, with a fantastic view of the sea. The original building was part of the 1929 World's Fair, but only part of the façade remains. However, the large garden with its old orange trees is still here, and there's a new swimming pool. Each room has a spacious balcony where you can enjoy your breakfast (be sure to book one with a view of the sea!). The layout of the rooms is excellent, and the lobby is nice and airy. Everything is kept to a minimum, and furnished in a modern, classic design, using pleasant neutral colours of black, grey or beige. My favourite treat: to sit on the terrace in front of the lobby bar, drinking a glass of freshly squeezed orange juice and enjoying the amazing view. I also highly recommend the restaurant, where Marsa — one of the few female chefs around — is in charge of the kitchen. The service throughout the hotel is especially courteous and friendly.

Auf dem Berg Montjuïc und gleichzeitig nahe dem Zentrum mit fantastischem Blick über das Meer liegt das Hotel Miramar, das der bekannte spanische Architekt Oscar Tusquets entworfen hat. Vom originalen Bau, der hier 1929 zur Weltausstellung errichtet worden war, steht nur noch ein Teil der Fassade. Aber der große Garten mit alten Orangenbäumen blieb erhalten, ein großer Pool wurde hinzugefügt. Jedes Zimmer besitzt einen großzügigen Balkon, auf dem es sich wunderbar frühstücken lässt – reservieren Sie am besten Meerblick! Die gut geschnittenen Räume und die luftige Lobby sind minimal und mit modernen Klassikern ausgestattet, alles ist in angenehmen Nicht-Farben wie Schwarz, Grau oder Beige gehalten. Ich liebe es besonders, auf der Terrasse vor der Lobby-Bar einen frischen Orangensaft zu trinken und die herrliche Aussicht zu genießen. Auch das Restaurant ist äußerst empfehlenswert – dort kocht Carme Marsa, einer der wenigen weiblichen Chefs –, und im ganzen Haus ist der Service überdurchschnittlich freundlich.

Conçu par l'architecte espagnol Oscar Tusquets, l'hôtel AC Miramar se dresse sur la colline du Montjuïc près du centre et offre une vue fantastique sur la mer. Il ne subsiste du bâtiment original édifié en 1929 dans le cadre de l'Exposition universelle qu'une partie de la façade. Mais le vaste jardin planté de vieux orangers a été conservé, une grande piscine y a été construite. Chaque chambre dispose d'un vaste balcon sur lequel il est merveilleux de prendre son petit déjeuner – surtout réservez une chambre avec vue sur la mer ! Les chambres bien dessinées et le hall aéré sont aménagés sobrement de classiques modernes dans des tons de noir, de gris ou de beige. J'aime particulièrement boire un jus d'orange frais pressé sur la terrasse du bar et admirer la vue magnifique. Je recommande aussi chaudement le restaurant – Carme Marsa, un des rares chefs féminins y est aux fourneaux. Dans toute la maison l'amabilité du personnel est supérieure à la moyenne.

Rates: Single and double rooms from 210 €, suites from 385 €. Breakfast 25 €.
Rooms: 75 rooms and suites.
Cuisine: The restaurant Forestier offers light Catalan cuisine with a subtle French touch – excellent.
History: The hotel was reopened in 2006.
X-Factor: My favourite hotel in Barcelona.
Internet: One hour for 6.50 €, 24 hours for 12 € (WLAN, high-speed).

Preise: EZ/DZ ab 210 €, Suite ab 385 €. Frühstück 25 €.
Zimmer: 75 Zimmer und Suiten.
Küche: Im Restaurant Forestier steht leichte katalanische Küche mit französischem Touch auf der Karte – hervorragend.
Geschichte: Das Haus wurde 2006 neu eröffnet.
X-Faktor: Mein Lieblingshotel in Barcelona!
Internet: 1 Stunde 6,50 €, 24 Stunden 12 € (WLAN, highspeed).

Prix : Chambre simple/double à partir de 210 €, suite à partir de 385 €. Petit déjeuner 25 €.
Chambres : 75 chambres et suites.
Restauration : Sur la carte du restaurant « Forestier », cuisine légère « french touch » – super.
Histoire : La maison a été rouverte en 2006.
Le « petit plus » : Mon hôtel favori à Barcelone !
Internet : 1 heure 6,50 €, 24 heures 12 € (WLAN, haut débit).

1

2

3

1   Miró & architecture/Miró & Architektur/
    Miró & architecture

Fundació Joan Miró
Parc de Montjuïc s/n
08038 Barcelona
Tel: +34 93 443 94 70
Fax: +34 93 329 86 09
www.bcn.fjmiro.es
Tues–Sat 10am–7pm (October–June),
and 10am–8pm (July–September)
Metro: L1, L3, L8 Espanya; L2, L3 Paral·lel

A double delight: 300 paintings and 150
sculptures of the celebrated artist are
housed in a simply amazing building.
Completed in 1975 by Miró's friend, the
Catalan architect Josep Lluís Sert, the airy,
light-filled Fundació Joan Miró is beautifully situated in a park on Montjuïc. The
large, white walls are the perfect setting
for Miró's colourful paintings. The views
into the garden and of the city, and the
little courtyards inside and out, provide a
refreshing counterpoint to the impressive
art. Nowhere have I seen such a harmonious interplay of art, architecture and
nature.

Nicht nur die ausgestellten 300 Gemälde
und 150 Skulpturen des berühmten katalanischen Künstlers sind fantastisch – auch
das Gebäude ist einfach großartig: Es liegt
in einem Park auf dem Montjuïc, ist luftig
und lichtdurchflutet – der katalanische
Architekt und Freund Mirós, Josep Lluís
Sert, vollendete es 1975. Auf den großen,
weißen Wänden heben sich Mirós farbige
Gemälde eindrucksvoll ab. Ausblicke und
Durchblicke in den Garten und über die
Stadt, kleine Innenhöfe im Freien sowie
Atrien wirken beim Betrachten der Kunst
äußerst erfrischend. Ich habe ein so har-
monisches Zusammenspiel von Kunst,
Architektur und Natur noch nirgendwo
schöner erlebt.

Si les 300 tableaux et 150 sculptures du
célèbre artiste catalan exposés ici sont
fantastiques, le bâtiment est quant à lui
tout simplement magnifique : situé dans
un parc sur le Montjuïc, il est aéré et lumi-
neux – l'architecte catalan Josep Lluís
Sert, un ami de Miró, l'a achevé en 1975.

Les vastes murs blancs mettent en valeur
de manière saisissante les tableaux aux
couleurs vives de Miró ; la vue sur le jardin et
sur la ville, sur les petites cours intérieures
et les atriums est extrêmement rafraîchis-
sante quand on contemple des œuvres
d'art. Je n'ai encore trouvé nulle part
une telle interaction harmonieuse d'art,
d'architecture et de nature.

2   Traditional bodega/Traditionelle
    Bodega/Bodega traditionnelle

Quimet & Quimet
Carrer del Poeta Cabanyes 25
08004 Barcelona
Tel: +34 93 442 31 42
Tues–Sat 11am–4pm and 7pm–10.30pm,
Sun 11am–4pm
Metro: L2, L3 Paral·lel

This little old bodega is now in the hands
of the fifth generation of the same family,
and has been a popular place in the unpretentious Poble Sec neighbourhood for
more than 100 years. The patrons eat
while standing at the bar, if they manage to
get that close. The "Pica Pica" are delicious
little appetisers, and there are excellent
wines and cheeses.

Diese alte und kleine Bodega wird schon
in der fünften Generation von derselben
Familie betrieben und gehört seit mehr als
100 Jahren zu den Lieblingsadressen der
Bewohner des Poble Sec – eines unprä-
tentiösen Viertels von Barcelona. Hier isst
man im Stehen am Tresen (sofern man
überhaupt dorthin gelangt). Sehr lecker
sind die kleinen Häppchen „Pica Pica" zum
Aperitif. Zudem gibt es ausgezeichnete
Weine und Käsesorten.

Cette petite bodega ancienne qui appartient à la même famille depuis cinq
générations est depuis plus d'un siècle
l'une des adresses préférées des habitants de Poble Sec, un quartier sans
prétention de Barcelone. Ici on mange
debout au comptoir (dans la mesure où
on y a accès) ; les amuse-bouche « Pica
Pica » sont délicieux pour accompagner
l'apéritif. On y trouve aussi des vins et
des fromages excellents.

3   A fountain à la Las Vegas/Brunnen im
    Las-Vegas-Stil/Fontaine dans le style
    de Las Vegas

La Font Màgica de Montjuïc
Plaça Carles de Buïgas
08014 Barcelona
Tel: +34 93 291 40 42
http://fonts.bcn.es
October–April Fri/Sat 7pm–9pm, May–
September Thurs–Sun 8pm–11.30pm
Music show every 30 minutes.
Metro: L1, L3, L8 Espanya

The impressive 50m by 65m fountain on the
Plaça Carles de Buïgas was built in 1929
for the World's Fair. The best time to see it
is on a summer evening, when colourfully
illuminated water jets dance in rhythm with
the music of Abba or Tchaikovsky.

Der imposante, 50 mal 65 Meter große
Brunnen mitten auf der Plaça Carles de
Buïgas wurde 1929 zur Weltausstellung
gebaut. Vor allem im Sommer sollte man
sich das abendliche Vergnügen nicht entgehen lassen, wenn zu Klängen von Abba
oder Tschaikowsky farbig angeleuchtete
Wasserjets im Rhythmus der Musik tanzen.

La fontaine magique de la Plaça Carles
de Buïgas, avec son bassin imposant de
50 sur 65 mètres, a été édifiée en 1929
à l'occasion de l'Exposition universelle.
Les soirs d'été surtout il ne faut pas rater
le spectacle, lorsque les jets d'eau illumi-
nés en couleur dansent au rythme de la
musique de Tchaïkovski ou d'Abba.

4   Almond milk & nougat/Mandelmilch &
    Nougat/Lait d'amandes & nougat

Horchatería Sirvent
Carrer del Parlament 56
08015 Barcelona
Tel: +34 93 441 27 20
www.turronessirvent.com
Daily 10am–9pm
Metro: L2 Sant Antoni

This shop, established in 1920, is located
in the very enjoyable Poble Sec district. In
summer, the residents queue up to order a

© akg-images / Erich Lessing

4

5

6

glass of almond milk, which they then drink standing up. The milk is a blend of "chufas" (tiger nuts), water and a little sugar and tastes very refreshing. On top of that, Tomás Sirvent is well known for his "turrones" (nougat), also made of almonds. You should try the nougat – either the soft "turrón de Xixona" or the hard variety, "Alicante". Note: almonds are very healthy!

Dieser Laden im sympathischen Poble Sec wurde 1920 gegründet. Hier stehen die Barceloneser im Sommer Schlange, um ein Glas „Órxata" zu bestellen und gleich im Stehen zu trinken. Die Milch wird aus „chufas" (Erdmandeln), Wasser und etwas Zucker gemixt und schmeckt sehr erfrischend. Tomás Sirvent ist zudem für seine „turrones" (Nougats) bekannt, die ebenfalls aus Mandeln gemacht werden. Probieren Sie entweder den weichen „turrón de Xixona" oder die harte Version „Alicante". Übrigens: Mandeln sind sehr gesund!

Ce magasin situé dans le quartier sympathique de Poble Sec date de 1920. L'été les Barcelonais y font la queue pour commander une orxata bue sur place. Ce lait préparé avec des « chufas » (des amandes de terre, fruit du souchet), de l'eau et un peu de sucre est très rafraîchissant. Tomás Sirvent est aussi connu pour ses « turrones » (tourons), à base d'amandes. Goûtez soit le tendre « turrón de Xixona » ou la version dure « Alicante ». Et n'oubliez pas que les amandes sont bonnes pour la santé.

5   Architecture/Architektur/Architecture

Pavelló Mies van der Rohe
Avinguda del Marquès de Comillas s/n
08038 Barcelona
Tel: +34 93 423 40 16
www.miesbcn.com
Metro: L1, L3 Espanya

Mies van der Rohe designed this little pavilion as the German contribution to the 1929 World's Fair. Today it is one of the most important buildings of the 20th century, and the chair designed for the building is one of the world's most famous. The original pavilion was destroyed after the fair, but an exact replica was built

from 1983 to 1986. The radically simplified architecture, the clear straight lines, a reflecting pool and the use of precious materials like onyx make this place a very special architectural experience. In my opinion, it's the most beautiful building in the world.

Mies van der Rohe entwarf diesen kleinen Pavillon als deutschen Beitrag zur Weltausstellung 1929 – er ist heute eines der wichtigsten Gebäude des 20. Jahrhunderts (und der für den Bau designte Stuhl einer der berühmtesten Sessel). Der ursprüngliche Pavillon wurde nach der Ausstellung zerstört, dann aber 1983–1986 detailgetreu rekonstruiert. Die radikal einfache Architektur aus reduzierten geraden Linien, einem reflektierenden Wasserbassin und edlen Materialien wie Onyx machen diesen Ort zu einem Architekturerlebnis erster Klasse. Für mich das schönste Gebäude der Welt.

Ce petit pavillon conçu par Mies van der Rohe, qui représentait l'Allemagne à l'Exposition universelle de 1929 est aujourd'hui l'un des bâtiments majeurs du XXe siècle (et la chaise Barcelone de Mies est devenue un classique). Le pavillon original, démoli après l'Exposition, a été reconstruit dans le détail de 1983 à 1986. L'architecture radicalement simple aux lignes droites, un bassin réfléchissant et des matériaux nobles comme l'onyx font de cet endroit une expérience architecturale super enrichissante. Pour moi, c'est le plus beau bâtiment du monde.

6   Panoramic-view restaurant/Panorama-
       Restaurant/Restaurant panoramique

Torre d'Alta Mar
Passeig de Joan de Borbó 88
08039 Barcelona
Tel: +34 93 221 00 07
www.torredealtamar.com
Daily 1pm–3.30pm and 7pm–11.30pm
Metro: L4 Barceloneta

Getting there is half the fun. Near the Hotel Miramar, you can take the cable car down to the base station in Raval, then walk to Torre de Sant Sebastià, once a

cable-car tower, and take the lift up 75 metres. From there you have an unbelievable 360-degree view and fresh, wonderfully prepared seafood. Warning: it's pricey.

Der Weg ist das Ziel: In der Nähe des Hotels Miramar kann man mit der Furnicular zur Talstation im Raval hinabschweben, zum Torre de Sant Sebastià laufen (einem ehemaligen Seilbahnwagenturm) und mit dem Lift in 75 Meter Höhe fahren. Oben genießt man dann ein unvergessliches 360-Grad-Panorama und frische, gut zubereitete Meeresfrüchte. Dieses Erlebnis hat allerdings seinen Preis.

À proximité de l'Hotel Miramar on peut s'envoler en funiculaire jusqu'à la station de la vallée du Raval, marcher jusqu'à la Torre de Sant Sebastià (une ancienne tour de funiculaire) et prendre l'ascenseur. Arrivé au but, 75 mètres plus haut, on admire une vue panoramique inoubliable tout en savourant des fruits de mer bien préparés. Mais les bonnes choses ont leur prix.

Personal discoveries/Eigene Entdeckungen/Découvertes personnelles :

_____

_____

_____

_____

_____

_____

_____

_____

_____

_____

Tibidabo

208 Gran Hotel La Florida

Gran Hotel La Florida

Carretera de Vallvidrera al Tibidabo, 83-93   08035 Barcelona
☎ +34 93 259 30 00   🖷 +34 93 259 30 01
info@hotellaflorida.com   www.hotellaflorida.com
The easiest way to reach the hotel is by taxi
(approx. 15–20 €) from downtown.
Booking: www.great-escapes-hotels.com

Gran Hotel La Florida

This impressive villa, designed by Ramon Raventós in 1925, is magnificently situated atop the Tibidabo mountain, only 15 minutes from the city centre. Always a meeting place for the city's high society, it has a list of celebrity guests that includes Ernest Hemingway, Rock Hudson and James Stewart. La Florida remained empty for many years, but it was recently modernised, refurbished and reopened in 2003 as a five-star hotel. They've kept the classic elegance of the hotel's original Art Déco and Art Nouveau design, and balanced it nicely with rooms that have a modern touch. Eight artists, including Rebecca Horn, have created "designer suites". All the rooms have extremely comfortable beds, as well as huge bathrooms (with the largest showers I have ever seen!). The inside and outside pools are so large that you can swim your daily lengths with ease. But the real luxury at this hotel is the breathtaking view that stretches to the horizon – fantastic by day or night.

Eine Viertelstunde vom Zentrum entfernt und auf der Spitze des Tibidabo thront diese imposante Villa, die Ramon Raventós 1925 baute. Hier traf sich die feine Gesellschaft der Stadt, und auch Ernest Hemingway, Rock Hudson sowie James Stewart zählten zu den Gästen. Später stand das La Florida jahrzehntelang leer, ehe es saniert und 2003 als 5-Sterne-Hotel wiedereröffnet wurde. Man hat versucht, den klassischen Stil beizubehalten (eine Mischung aus Art déco und Art nouveau), ihm aber zugleich einen modernen Twist zu geben: So wurden acht „Designersuiten" von Künstlern gestaltet, unter ihnen Rebecca Horn. Alle Zimmer bieten besonders bequeme Betten sowie riesige Bäder, deren Duschen größer sind als alle, die ich bisher gesehen habe. Auch der Innen- und Außenpool sind von eindrucksvoller Länge, sodass man hier richtig Bahnen ziehen kann. Doch der wirkliche Luxus ist der atemberaubende Ausblick bis zum Horizont – bei Tag und Nacht gigantisch.

Cette villa imposante construite en 1925 par Ramon Raventós trône au sommet du pic Tibidabo, à un quart d'heure du centre-ville. Elle était le rendez-vous du beau monde et Ernest Hemingway, Rock Hudson, James Stewart y ont souvent séjourné. Plus tard La Florida est restée vide pendant des décennies avant d'être rénovée et de rouvrir en 2003. Dans le nouvel hôtel cinq étoiles, on a essayé de préserver le style classique, mariage d'Art nouveau et d'Art Déco, en le modernisant. Huit « designer-suits » ont été ainsi décorées par des artistes dont Rebecca Horn. Les chambres offrent des lits particulièrement confortables et des salles de bains gigantesques – je n'avais jamais vu de cabines de douches aussi spacieuses. La piscine intérieure et la piscine extérieure sont elles aussi d'une grandeur impressionnante et on peut vraiment y faire ses longueurs. Mais le vrai luxe c'est la vue exceptionnelle – jour et nuit prodigieuse – sur la ville et la mer.

Rates: Single and double rooms from 400 €, suites from 775 €. Breakfast 28 €.
Rooms: 74 rooms and suites.
Cuisine: Catalan and Mediterranean dishes are served in the restaurant L'Orangerie.
History: In the '50s, the hotel was the in-place for the rich and famous. It stood empty from 1979 to 2001, then was refurbished and reopened in 2003.
X-Factor: The Zen-like spa.
Internet: One hour for 10 € (with a credit card) or 12.50 € (with a voucher; broadband and WLAN, high-speed).

Preise: EZ/DZ ab 400 €, Suite ab 775 €. Frühstück 28 €.
Zimmer: 74 Zimmer und Suiten.
Küche: Im Restaurant L'Orangerie bekommt man katalanische und mediterrane Menüs.
Geschichte: Das Hotel galt in den 1950ern als *place to be* der High Society. 1979–2001 stand es leer, dann wurde es renoviert und 2003 neu eröffnet.
X-Faktor: Das Spa mit Zen-Ambiente.
Internet: 1 Stunde 10 € (Kreditkarte) bzw. 12,50 € (Voucher; Breitband und WLAN, highspeed).

Prix : Chambre simple/double à partir de 400 €, suite à partir de 775 €. Petit déjeuner 28 €.
Chambres : 74 chambres et suites.
Restauration : « L'Orangerie » propose des plats catalans et méditerranéens.
Histoire : Très en vogue dans la haute société au cours des années 1950, l'hôtel est resté vide de 1979 à 2001 avant d'être rénové et rouvert en 2003.
Le « petit plus » : Le spa et son ambiance zen.
Internet : 1 heure 10 € (carte de crédit) ou 12,50 € (coupon ; bande large et WLAN, haut débit).

1

2

3

1   Amusement park/Vergnügungspark/
Parc d'attractions

Parc d'Atraccions del Tibidabo
Plaça del Tibidabo 3-4
08035 Barcelona
Tel: +34 93 211 79 42
www.tibidabo.es
July/August Wed–Fri & Sun midday–9pm
or 10pm, Sat midday–11pm. Restricted
opening hours in other months. (Check
their website.)
Metro: Furnicular del Tibidabo; Tibi Bus
from Plaça Catalunya to Tibidabo

This quaint, old-fashioned amusement
park is just a short walk away from Gran
Hotel La Florida. Situated on the side of
the mountain at an altitude of 512 metres,
just below the neo-Gothic church Sagrat
Cor (modelled on Sacré Cœur in Paris)
and right next to Norman Foster's famous
Torre de Collserola television tower, the
park has a publicly accessible viewing
platform. The park still has some old
amenities that date from its establishment
in 1901. Filled with charm and nostalgia,
it makes an entertaining outing not only for
children, but also for the young at heart.
The panoramic view over the city and the
sea is unbeatable.

Dieser altmodische Vergnügungspark ist
nur einen Spaziergang vom Gran Hotel
La Florida entfernt. Er liegt auf 512 Me-
tern Höhe, unterhalb der neugotischen
Kirche Sagrat Cor (Sacré-Cœur in Paris
war das Vorbild) und neben dem berühmten
Fernsehturm Torre de Collserola von
Norman Foster mit einer öffentlich zugäng-
lichen Aussichtsplattform (auch eine
Attraktion). Der Park wurde 1901 eingeweiht und besitzt noch heute ältere
Einrichtungen (zum Teil sogar aus seiner
Gründungszeit) – er hat einen ganz eige-
nen, nostalgischen Charme und ist ein
lustiges Ausflugsziel auch für Erwachsene,
die Kind geblieben sind. Außerdem eröffnet er wunderschöne Panoramen über
die Stadt und das Meer.

Du Gran Hotel La Florida, une petite pro-
menade nous mène dans ce parc d'attractions désuet, situé à 515 m d'altitude en

dessous de l'église néogothique Sagrat
Cor (le Sacré-Cœur de Montmartre lui a
servi de modèle) et à côté de la célèbre
tour de télévision Torre de Collserola de
Norman Foster dotée d'une plate-forme
d'observation accessible au public (une
autre attraction). Le parc a été inauguré en
1901 et certaines de ses attractions datent
encore de l'époque de sa création. Son
charme nostalgique très particulier fait de
lui un but de randonnée apprécié des adul-
tes qui ont gardé une âme d'enfant. En
outre, la vue sur la ville et la Méditerranée
y est spectaculaire.

2   Bar with a view/Bar mit Aussicht/
Bar avec vue

Mirablau
Plaça del Doctor Andreu
08035 Barcelona
Tel: +34 93 418 58 79
Daily 11am–5am.
Metro: L7 Avinguda Tibidabo

Located on Tibidabo mountain, at the
cable car terminal, this modest bar is
where the local residents meet to enjoy
the sunset. Or go there after dinner to
enjoy a breathtaking view of the lights of
Barcelona, while listening to a great selection of blues and soul music. The beauty of
it all makes you weak in the knees.

An der Endstation der Kabelbahn und am
Berghang des Tibidabo gelegen, ist diese
unspektakuläre Bar ein wunderbarer Platz,
an dem sich die Einheimischen treffen,
um den Sonnenuntergang zu erleben.
Oder man genießt nach dem Dinner bei
Blues- und Soulmusik eine atemberaubende Aussicht auf das Lichtermeer von
Barcelona. Zum Niederknien schön!

Situé sur le versant du Tibidabo au termi-
nus du funiculaire, ce bar sans prétention
est un endroit merveilleux où les autochtones se retrouvent pour regarder le
coucher du soleil. On peut aussi, le soir
après le dîner, écouter du blues et de la
soul en contemplant émerveillé la mer
de lumière de Barcelone. On s'agenouille-
rait devant.

3   Restaurant/Restaurant/Restaurant

Bestial
Carrer de Ramon Trias Fargas 2-4
08005 Barcelona
Tel: +34 93 224 04 07
www.bestialdeltragaluz.com
Mon-Fri 1pm–3.45pm and 8pm–11.30pm
(Fri to 12.30am), Sat 1pm–4.30pm and
8pm–12.30am, Sun 1pm–4.30pm and
8pm–11pm.
Metro: L4 Ciutadella Vila Olímpica
(Map on page 110)

If you get too lonesome in Gran Hotel
La Florida, go down to the lowest point in
Barcelona – down to the sea and into
Bestial. It's a good idea to wait for a table
out on the terrace before settling into this
restaurant with its minimalist ambience
and fantastic view. Make your way through
the excellent menu, which has a touch
of Italian influence. Recently, several
nightclubs have opened nearby, so there's
somewhere to go after dinner.

Wem es auf dem Tibidabo im Gran Hotel
La Florida zu einsam wird, der fährt hinab
zum niedrigsten Punkt der Stadt: direkt
ans Meer und ins Bestial. Dort wartet man
am besten auf einen Platz auf der Terrasse, um sich in minimalistischem Ambiente
und bei tollem Ausblick durch die feine,
italienisch angehauchte Speisekarte zu
essen. Nur wenige Meter entfernt haben
einige Nachtclubs eröffnet, sodass auch
für Unterhaltung nach dem Dinner ge-
sorgt ist.

Si on se sent trop seul au Gran Hotel
La Florida en haut du Tibidabo, on peut
descendre en ville, et aller au « Bestial »,
en bord de mer. Ici le mieux est d'attendre
une place en terrasse, avant de se régaler
de fines spécialités qui fleurent bon l'Italie
dans un décor épuré tout en admirant la
vue. Quelques boîtes de nuit ont ouvert
à quelques mètres d'ici, si bien qu'il ne
faut pas se faire de soucis pour savoir où
passer la soirée.

4

5

4   Park & museum/Park & Museum/
     Park & Musée

Casa Museu Gaudí/Parc Güell
08035 Barcelona
Tel: +34 93 219 38 11
www.casamuseugaudi.org
April–September 10am–7.45pm,
October–March 10am–5.45pm.
Metro: L3 Lesseps

With a commission from the industrialist
Eusebi Güell, Gaudí created this park
between 1900 and 1914. It has been a
UNESCO World Heritage site since 1964.
The renowned architect ensured that the
work was conducted in a way that was both
environmentally sound and inexpensive.
He took the materials from the site itself
and used broken pots and pieces from the
nearby ceramic factory for the mosaics.
Gaudí's own house, where he lived from
1906 until his death in 1926, is also here,
and it has been converted into a museum.
This is the place to combine sightseeing
with a walk in the countryside.

Gaudí schuf diesen Park zwischen 1900
und 1914 im Auftrag des Industriellen
Eusebi Güell. Beim Bau achtete der
berühmte Architekt auf umweltgerechtes
und kostengünstiges Arbeiten – die Materialien fand er auf dem Gelände selbst,
und für die vielen Mosaike verwendete er
Abfälle aus den nahen Keramikfabriken.
Der Park beherbergt auch das Wohnhaus
Gaudís, in dem dieser von 1906 bis zu
seinem Tod 1926 lebte. Heute dient es als
Museum. Seit 1984 gehört der Park zum
UNESCO-Weltkulturerbe. Hier kann man
einen Spaziergang im Grünen mit vielen
Sehenswürdigkeiten verbinden.

Gaudí a créé ce parc entre 1900 et 1914
à la demande de l'industriel Eusebi Güell,
veillant à ce que les constructions soient
écologiques et bon marché – il trouva les
matériaux sur place et utilisa les déchets
des usines de céramique toutes proches
pour réaliser les nombreuses mosaïques.
Le parc abrite aussi la maison, aujourd'hui
transformée en musée, dans laquelle le
célèbre architecte vécut de 1906 à sa
mort, en 1926. Le parc figure depuis 1984

sur la liste du patrimoine mondial de
l'UNESCO. Ici on peut se promener dans
la verdure en voyant beaucoup de choses
intéressantes.

5   Restaurant/Restaurant/Restaurant

Botafumeiro
Carrer Gran de Gràcia 81
08012 Barcelona
Tel: +34 93 218 42 30
www.botafumeiro.es
Mon–Sun 1pm–1am.
Metro: L3 Fontana

This restaurant is where Barcelona's
locals meet for a fine late supper after
viewing an exhibition, or attending a concert. The hottest seats are those "en la
barra" (at the bar), but the elegant wood-
panelled rooms are also very pleasant to
sit in and eat fish or seafood prepared in
the northern Spanish style. The restaurant
is so genteel that the menu given to ladies
doesn't list the prices – a nod to bygone
days.

In diesem Restaurant treffen sich die
Barceloneser gerne nach dem Besuch
einer Ausstellung oder eines Konzertes
zum gepflegten späten Dinner. Besonders
begehrt sind die Plätze „en la barra" (an
der Bar); aber auch in den eleganten,
holzvertäfelten Räumen sitzt man sehr gut
und bestellt Fisch und Meeresfrüchte nach
nordspanischen Rezepten. Es ist hier so
vornehm, dass die Menükarten, die den
Damen überreicht werden, keine Preise
beinhalten. Diese sehen nur die Herren
auf ihrer Version – eine Hommage an die
alten Zeiten.

Les Barcelonais se retrouvent volontiers
ici le soir pour dîner après avoir visité une
exposition ou écouté un concert. Les
places « en la barra » (au bar) sont particulièrement convoitées, mais les élégantes
salles lambrissées dans lesquelles on peut
déguster des spécialités de poisson et de
fruits de mer typiques du nord de l'Espagne,
sont également très accueillantes. Dans
ce restaurant très distingué, les dames se
voient remettre une carte sans prix – un
hommage au bon vieux temps.

MUSEUMS, ARCHITECTURE, GALLERIES, ETC.

© 2007 TASCHEN GmbH
Hohenzollernring 53, D-50672 Köln
www.taschen.com

Compilation, Editing, Writing & Layout by
Angelika Taschen, Berlin

General Project Manager
Stephanie Bischoff, Cologne

Photos
Pep Escoda, Tarragona

Cover Illustration
Olaf Hajek, www.olafhajek.com

Maps
dieSachbearbeiter.*innen*, Berlin

Graphic Design
Eggers + Diaper, Berlin

Lithograph Manager
Thomas Grell, Cologne

French Translation
Thérèse Chatelain-Südkamp, Cologne
Michèle Schreyer, Cologne

English Translation
Kate Chapman, Berlin

Printed in Italy
ISBN 978-3-8365-0047-0